Anarchy, Order, and Integration

Anarchy, Order, and Integration

How to Manage Interdependence

HARVEY STARR

Ann Arbor

THE UNIVERSITY OF MICHIGAN PRESS

Copyright © by the University of Michigan 1997
All rights reserved
Published in the United States of America by
The University of Michigan Press
Manufactured in the United States of America
⊗ Printed on acid-free paper

2000   1999   1998   1997   4   3   2   1

A CIP catalog record for this book is available from the British Library.

Library of Congress Cataloging-in-Publication Data

Starr, Harvey.
    Anarchy, order, and integration : how to manage interdependence /
Harvey Starr.
        p.   cm.
    Includes bibliographical references and index.
    ISBN 0-472-10849-2 (alk. paper)
    1. International relations—Philosophy.   2. International
cooperation.   3. International organization.   4. World politics.
I. Title.
JX1395.S7184   1997
327.1'01—dc21   97-4790
                                                                            CIP

To my father, and
To the memory of my mother

Contents

Preface and Acknowledgments

As with all intellectual endeavors that develop over a period of time, there are innumerable individuals who have influenced the thinking that has gone into this book. The initial versions of the various chapters were written at different times and benefited from the comments and reactions of quite different sets of people and audiences. Though too large a group to name, you know who you are, and I thank you. This group includes the many graduate students who were seminar participants in several sections of International Relations Theory at the University of South Carolina, as well as the hardy crew of Masters in International Relations (MAIR) students at the Australian National University who took the International Relations Theory course from me in the March 1996 term.

However, several people must be singled out for special recognition. Mike McGinnis at Indiana University and Don Puchala at South Carolina both took the time to look at the initial manuscript and give me comments, or listen to my pitch and help me examine my ideas through discussion. Lin Ostrom at Indiana also provided feedback on the original prospectus. Randolph Siverson at the University of California, Davis, and Chuck Kegley at South Carolina were frequent, and helpful, sounding boards for various ideas; Chuck was of particular help for the paper that was the original version of chapter 6. Finally, Bruce Russett deserves special mention for the constant flow of ideas, suggestions, and papers and for his important input and contribution to the sections of this book whose original versions were initially part of our coauthored textbook, *World Politics: The Menu for Choice* (4th ed. [1992] and 5th ed. [1996]).

This book would never have happened without the help of Colin Day, director of the University of Michigan Press. The initial interest, support, and encouragement of Malcolm Litchfield (then at UMP) were especially important to the development and completion of this project. This encouragement was continued by Charles Myers. His comments, and those of UMP's referees, were important in the revision of the final manuscript. Despite the best efforts of all these individuals to save me, any weaknesses in presentation, logic, or argument are my responsibility alone.

I would like to acknowledge the support of the University of South

Carolina, which furnished me with a sabbatical in the spring semester of 1996. I would also like to thank the Department of International Relations, the Research School of Pacific and Asian Studies, at the Australian National University for affording me a congenial setting for revising parts of this manuscript as well as an environment for crisp discussion of IR theory. Especial thanks go to Andy Mack, head of the department, as well as John Ravenhill, Greg Fry, and Jim Richardson.

Much of the material in Part 1 of this book is based upon, and has developed from, material appearing in the fourth and fifth editions of Bruce Russett and Harvey Starr, *World Politics: The Menu for Choice* (New York: W. H. Freeman). Again, thanks go to Bruce Russett as well as Susan Brennan of W. H. Freeman for their support of this project. An earlier version of chapter 5 appeared as "How to Manage Interdependence? The State in a Multi–Centric/Transnational World," discussant paper prepared for the session on Political Perspectives and International Business at the conference on Perspectives on International Business: Theory, Research, and Institutional Arrangements, May 21–23, 1992, at the University of South Carolina. Chapter 6 was based on an earlier version that appeared as "International Law and International Order" in Charles W. Kegley Jr., ed., *Controversies in International Relations Theory: Realism and the Neoliberal Challenge* (New York: St. Martin's Press, 1995), 299–315. Portions of chapter 7 were based on material originally appearing in "Democracy and War: Choice, Learning, and Security Communities," *Journal of Peace Research* 29 (1992): 207–13; and "Why Don't Democracies Fight Each Other? Evaluating the Theory-Findings Feedback Loop," *Jerusalem Journal of International Relations* 14 (1992): 41–59.

CHAPTER 1

Introduction

Interdependence and Order: What Is to Be Investigated

Most observers agree that the global arena is in the midst of multiple changes; that we are in an era of "turbulence," to use the terminology popularized by James Rosenau. This era has been characterized by a series of "posts": post–cold war politics and security issues, postindustrial states, the post–Maastricht structure of Europe, and of course, postmodern society. The elements that create and intensify global interdependencies have also been expanding rapidly, generating questions about the viability of the state and the viability of the statecentric system that has existed for over half a millennium, as well as what sorts of structures and behaviors might replace them. In thinking about such changes, it is important to understand what is new and what is constant—what has been fundamentally altered and what are simply new forms of more routine patterns and phenomena in the international sphere.[1]

To address these questions usefully and thoughtfully, the student of international relations or world politics must have a firm understanding of the "nature" of the international system and the "nature" of *order* within it. Even though there is a substantial amount of extant work on order within the anarchic system—which seems to be growing exponentially—my feeling is that too much of it has been situated within an overly narrow theoretical debate involving Realism and Neorealism, as they refine or contend with each other or various forms of Liberalism. One purpose of this book is to expand the conceptual boundaries of that debate through the introduction of opportunity and willingness, interdependence, integration, and adaptation. By so expanding the debate—and questioning Lib-

---

1. What is new or constant is raised by Kegley (1995) but is also the question raised by Robert Jervis (1991–92) in *his* consideration of global futures. What has or has not changed is also crucial to understanding whether or not, or to what extent, we have undergone what Nijman (1993, 127) has called a "geopolitical transition"—"the transitory stage between two more or less stable geopolitical orders. A stable political order is characterized by a predictability of events that results from the presence of well-established geopolitical codes . . ." which are foreign policy goals and strategies that guide state behavior.

eralism as well as the Realism-Neorealism relationship—I hope to highlight the artificiality of the Realist-Liberal spectrum that has come to dominate much of our thinking about international politics.

Additionally, too much of the extant work on order within the anarchic system has been focused on thinking about short–term foreign policy
options or policy analysis. A good deal of this writing has become a quasi-
journalistic commentary, which is part of the "quest for things to worry
about" (Mueller 1994, 1995, chap. 1). That is, by shifting definitions, by
elevating smaller problems to major ones, and by raising the standards
used to judge the existence and quality of current or future
stability/peace/order, many commentators have approached the topic of
global order as a *new* problem that defies solution; "that international
affairs had somehow become especially tumultuous, unstable, and complex" (Mueller 1995, 13). A second purpose of this book, as previously
introduced, is to look at what is actually new and what is constant and how
international actors have adapted to the context created by both.

To do so, I prefer to start with Hedley Bull's (1977, 24) observation
that "order is part of the historical record of international relations," and
with K. J. Holsti's (1992, 31) brief characterization of order: "Order
implies limits on behavior. In a society of states, these limitations are
spelled out in international law, the conventions of diplomacy, the balance
of power, and even in war, when it is used to enforce community norms."

This view of order includes most of the components of what scholars
have come to call "regimes"—the "governance" of areas of international
interaction through norms, rules, law, and organizations (ideas that will be
more fully addressed in chapters 3, 4, and 6). Even more important, Holsti's characterization includes Bull's (1977) focus on the relationship
between "order" and "society." Holsti's view includes most of the phenomena that Bull feels must be investigated in dealing with international
order. Zacher (1992, 60) is one of many who agree on the importance of
Bull's work: "the character of the international system is much better captured by Hedley Bull's concept of 'the anarchical society' than it is by Kenneth Waltz's notion of 'anarchy.'"[2]

However, by focusing on "order" as a new problem, or as a condition
now under exceptionally high degrees of stress, most of the current writing
on order, stability, and the global system fails to utilize a number of rather
important concepts and theoretical constructs found in the international
relations literature. Broader themes—such as interdependence, order,

---

2. While I hope to draw in additional phenomena from multidisciplinary perspectives
on order in the international system, Bull's *The Anarchical Society* (1977) is a must for the
reader with little background on the history and nature of the international system, the society of states, and the order that exists within that society.

society, and collective or common interests, all investigated within a broad, adaptive agent-structure framework such as opportunity and willingness—are necessary for systematic and analytic thinking about global politics. Given that much of the extant commentary is policy oriented and written by specialists in "international security," I do not find it surprising that most such writing fails to include the theoretical bases noted as necessary for our full understanding. It is important to realize that the theoretical bases I have identified are also crucial in *critiquing* Realist analyses of systemic anarchy and the behavior of sovereign states.[3]

The book that follows (which draws upon and expands ideas I have developed in past work) will provide an overview of what I feel are the necessary themes and theoretical issues in regard both to Realism and to alternative approaches that stress the shortcomings of Realism. These themes and issues are summarized by the question found in the subtitle of this volume: How to manage interdependence? As we shall see, Realists (and Structural Realists) have one answer to "how to manage interdependence?" based on security and military capabilities and mercantilist economic variations; an answer that is quite incomplete. Neorealist answers that focus on international regimes, while richer and more relevant, are also incomplete.

Elements of both must be incorporated, along with major components of the "Neoliberal challenge," which is derived from a rediscovered Wilsonian Liberalism (see esp. Kegley 1995; Rosenau and Czempiel 1992). Indeed, I wish to stake out a middle position between Realist beliefs, such as those that accord all significance to the state, and those transnational/Liberal beliefs that hold that the state is essentially irrelevant. I hope to do so through a focus on interdependence and its relationship to chang-

---

3. Let me digress briefly to provide one example. Cioffi-Revilla and Starr (1995) present formal analyses demonstrating that opportunity and willingness are jointly necessary conditions for any behavior to occur. Thus, opportunity and willingness can be represented by the conjunctive Boolean AND indicating joint necessity. A counterfactual world of the Boolean OR, where *only one condition*—either opportunity or willingness would be necessary—would be quite different: where only wishing for something would make it so, or merely having the capacity to do something would make it so. Cioffi-Revilla and Starr (1995, 454) then observe:

> For example, many of the pathologies of thinking about world politics stem from the failure to understand, or distinguish the world of AND (causal conjunction or necessity) from the world of OR (causal disjunction or sufficiency). One example is the use of worst-case scenarios by analysts based only on the capabilities of opponents (opportunity), and either ignoring intentions (willingness) or assuming that capabilities offer a rational basis for *inferring* intentions. In essence, such analyses are based on the counterfactual, unreal world that has a disjunctive OR . . . Not surprisingly, many national security policies based on worst-case scenarios fail, or produce opposite results. . . . (emphasis in original)

ing global contexts, issues, and conditions—and how such change has affected the mechanisms states have used to manage that interdependence. Such mechanisms also sit in a middle ground—they represent neither the mechanisms of power politics nor the utopian promise of extreme Idealists.

The question of how to manage interdependence will shape my approach to these themes and issues. I will address them by: (1) delineating the primary tension that exists between the formal anarchy of the Westphalian system (including the sovereignty of the states that compose it) and the interdependence that characterizes all systems; (2) presenting the component concepts and phenomena of the "Westphalian trade-off" between autonomy and interdependence; and (3) how order operates within such a context.

The central theme of this book is that the global system can best be understood as the consequence of states *adapting* to changing interdependencies. States *do* remain important in this system, but the reality they adapt to is changing. Thus, the environment surrounding states is important—*not* because it is "anarchic," as argued by Structural Realists such as Waltz (1979), but because environmental conditions have changed, thereby changing the meaning and significance of such structural characteristics as "anarchy." The most crucial aspect to the approach to world order presented in this book is the explicit recognition of complex feedback loops—that the modes by which states adapt lead to changes in both the states themselves and in their environment (see also Friedman and Starr forthcoming). Examples of these phenomena can be clearly seen in the study of integration and in the growing transformation of states to democratic forms of governance.

The central theme of adaptation is thus firmly embedded within the agency-structure question: the relationship between actor and context or between entity and environment that is essential to any investigation of social behavior. The agency-structure framework used here will draw upon the concepts of opportunity and willingness that I have developed to organize my thinking about international politics. It will come as no surprise to readers familiar with my other work that the opportunity-and-willingness framework, which draws on the theoretic constructs of Harold and Margaret Sprout, plays a leading role in the book to follow.[4]

Opportunity and willingness draws upon the "ecological triad" of the Sprouts: entity, environment, and entity-environment relationship. As with any agent-structure approach, opportunity and willingness reveal the

4. See particularly Most and Starr 1989, Siverson and Starr 1991, Cioffi-Revilla and Starr 1995, and Friedman and Starr forthcoming. Note that this particular summary statement of my central theme in the text benefited from the comments of Mike McGinnis.

complexity and uncertainty in international phenomena; a complexity adequately addressed by neither Realism, Neorealism, nor most variants of transnational liberalism. Yet, as Cioffi-Revilla and Starr (1995, 468) demonstrate, "the fundamental uncertainty of politics is scientifically tractable." With concepts such as "nice laws," "substitutability," context, and adaptation, the opportunity-and-willingness framework can deal with both the analytical and operational levels of theory and give us a better grasp of what behaviors are more or less likely to occur under what conditions.

Again, Cioffi-Revilla and Starr (1995, 417) demonstrate how such a framework or theory can distinguish "between the first-order *analytical* causes of political behavior (i.e., opportunity and willingness) and the second-order *operational* causes (the substitutable modes of opportunity and willingness). The latter refers to the actual tools of policy action taken from an actor's 'menu for choice'" (emphasis in original).

At the level of second-order operational tools of policy action, we will find the discussion repeatedly turning to *integration.* As the exemplar of how to manage interdependence in a "positive" manner (Russett and Starr 1996, 349), integration consequently becomes an important focus of our thinking about interdependence and order. It also provides the substantive and theoretical means by which to bring together regimes, international organizations, and international law and demonstrate their relevance in a world of sovereign states and formal anarchy. Significantly, integration studies provided the first substantive and theoretical challenge to the relevance and applicability of Realism. Just as significantly, integration theory also demonstrates that such a challenge is constituted by more than Liberal laissez-faire policies or Idealist reliance on international law.

New analyses will also be presented through the development of important linkages between research on "the democratic peace" and the older (and more powerful) work on integration theory. These linkages allow us to merge our thinking about the possibilities of stable zones of peace with our thinking about the conditions of interdependence: how interdependence can be managed positively to deal with the key interstate issue of conflict within the anarchic system.

The discussion of such linkages will be used as a jumping-off point for an assessment of the meaning and feasibility of a "new world order." A great deal of misdirected—and mushy—writing has been devoted to the concept of "new world order." The concluding chapter will be an attempt to rectify some of the problems in that thinking by directing our attention to the sorts of regulatory mechanisms needed to create and maintain order by the actors in a global system in an era of both new and increasingly numerous collective action problems. As the most extreme form of interdependencies, collective goods problems are basic to understanding the political institutions and practices that arise in a system: "Collective action problems . . . are foundational: were it not for collective action problems there would be no need for politics" (Taylor and Singleton 1993, 66).

How to Proceed: The Plan of the Book

I see this book as an opportunity to pull together, in a coherent whole, the various pieces to these puzzles that I have discussed previously; to amplify these discussions and expose them to a broader audience. I wish to use this book to present in a succinct manner the basic structure of my thinking about interdependence and global order. The book is *not* intended to to be a synoptic literature review or a comprehensive overview of international relations theory. It will not include syntheses of the vast (and continually growing) literature on world order and the future of the world system, nor will it synthesize the literatures that have been developed around the central phenomena to be discussed: interdependence, the international system and system change, anarchy and sovereignty, integration, international law, and regimes.

The book is organized into two parts. Part 1 introduces what I feel to be the basic building blocks for thinking about order in international relations, including the concepts of system, interdependence, transnational relations, regimes, and collective goods. I will discuss what these things mean and how they relate to one another, what issues they create, the tensions they generate in dealing with global problems, and general responses to such tensions. The theme of interdependence goes beyond simply giving lip service to complexity. It is used to indicate how the environment creates special types of incentive structures within which entities operate and how these structures create special problems that require creative modes of management.

Part 2 addresses several specific ways of thinking about and dealing with the tensions of the Westphalian trade-off:

state sovereignty and interdependence
the anarchic system and order through international law
the Realist perspective generated by the anarchic system and the contradictions to it found in integration theory and practice as well as in the peace among democracies

The concluding chapter will recapitulate the major themes of the book as well as extend them to a discussion of the prospects for a "new world order" in a global system of changing norms, developing regimes, and expanding democracy. I will attempt to present these discussions clearly, logically, and succinctly with a minimum of clutter. If successful, I might convince readers of different ways to view these central questions in the study of world politics. At a minimum, I would hope that readers would use this book as an opportunity to revisit their own views and submit them to explicit critical evaluation.

Part 1

CHAPTER 2

The Basics: Interdependence, Transnational Relations, and Order in an Anarchic System

If the central organizational question of this book is "how to manage interdependence?" then we must clarify this concept and several others. The theme of adaptation involves complex feedback loops, the nature of the environment or context, and the relationships between the entity and its environment. We thus need to introduce opportunity and willingness and the idea of the "menu" for choice. We must also spend some time with the basic idea of interdependence and why it is central to our thinking about order in the global system.

Some of these ideas and presentations will seem quite elementary or self-evident to the serious student of international relations theory. However, my aim here is to set out the building blocks I am using as clearly as possible, to be clear in my conceptualization of those phenomena and how I am linking them together. I want the reader to be clear as to my logic and how I arrive at my conclusions.

Opportunity and Willingness and the *Menu* for Choice

Interdependence is a quality of systems. Systems are composed of units of some kind and the interaction among them. In the simplest of terms, we must be concerned with each unit and how each unit adapts to its environment. This individual adaptation produces the patterns of interaction that characterize the system.[1] The basic *ecological triad* of Harold and Margaret Sprout (e.g., 1969) helps us think about units and their environments. The ecological triad is composed of three elements: (1) an actor, or entity, of some sort, (2) an environment that surrounds the entity, and (3) the entity-environment relationship.

---

1. I recognize that this set of simple assertions reflects a perspective quite at odds with Waltz's 1979 view of systems and his arguments against "reductionism." At this juncture, I wish only to direct the reader to a more detailed set of critiques of Waltz found in Most and Starr 1989 and Friedman and Starr forthcoming.

This seemingly elemental construct has served as the basis for the development of the opportunity-and-willingness framework. The ecological triad provides great utility in its ability to link the entity and the environment by helping us see how and why different environments constrain, limit, or enable what entities are able to do and what they are likely to do. The Sprouts were critical of the limitations of deterministic models. As a response to such deterministic approaches to international relations, which included Realist-geopolitical models (see Starr 1991a), the Sprouts presented alternative forms of the entity-environment relationship. Three of these are particularly useful to our thinking: *environmental possibilism,* where the environment is seen as a set of constraints on what is actually possible for the entity to do in the environment; *environmental probablism,* where the environmental constraints and possibilities make certain behaviors more or less likely; and *cognitive behaviorism,* where the entity—as ultimately embodied by individual decision makers—is linked to the environment through the images of the environment that people hold. The core of the Sprouts' alternatives to determinism is that the environment presents a set of possibilities that can be perceived by decision makers and that affect the probabilities that certain choices will be made.[2]

Thus, we may choose to study international phenomena from a "macro" or a "micro" perspective: Is it the international system that accounts for the behavior of its constituent state units, or is it the states (and their subunits) that account for variations in the international system? Do we look at the state or at its societal components—ethnic groups or classes or specific economic interests? Do we look at the government or at the bureaucracies that comprise it? Do we look at bureaucracies or at the individuals that comprise them? Do we look at the system or its constituent parts? From the Sproutian view—or the opportunity-and-willingness variant of the agent-structure perspective—we should look at *all* of these levels nested within one another. Hollis and Smith note (1990, 8), "At each stage the 'unit' of the higher level becomes the 'system' of the lower layer."

The macro, or inclusive, system forms the environment for its parts. As noted, the ultimate constituent parts, surrounded by a set of environments, are individuals who act as governmental decision makers. These decision makers in turn constantly endeavor, insofar as possible, to shape and control those environments. The macro approach tells one story, explaining what has occurred because of outside factors; the micro approach tells another story, attempting to understand the significance of

2. For an important discussion on the nature of context, how it can affect how environed units behave, and how we can study the entity-environment relationship, see Goertz 1994.

events from the point of view of people within the units. Again, Hollis and Smith (1990, 42) observe, "Whatever the unit, its activities can be explained from without or understood from within. Every unit has a decision-making process. Those making the decisions are influenced from outside and from inside." Ultimately, then, we are concerned with the possibilities and constraints that face decision makers (opportunity) and with the choices that they make in light of these possibilities and constraints (willingness).

Using the ideas of opportunity and willingness forces us to engage in both explanation and understanding (in the terms of Hollis and Smith). Opportunity and willingness force us to consider both the world system, or broader environment, and the process of decision making that goes on within that system's constituent units. The various levels of analysis involved in the analysis of international politics are thus linked by thinking of a decision maker as an entity who must behave within the very complex environment that surrounds him or her. Each level of analysis describes one of the environments within which the decision maker must operate.

Opportunity

The environments of decision-making entities provide a structure of opportunities, risks, and potential costs and benefits, constraining decision makers. How are all these elements captured by the concept of opportunity?

First, the environment makes certain opportunities, and not others, *possible.* Here the environment is seen as a set of constraints on what is actually possible for the entity to do in the environment; Goertz (1994) elaborates on this idea in his discussion of context as "barrier." Napoleon could not threaten Moscow with nuclear destruction; the Spanish in the eighth century could not draw upon the resources of the New World to repel the initial Islamic invasion of Iberia, because no European knew that there was a New World; the economically besieged countries trying to deal with the Great Depression of the 1930s could not call on the International Monetary Fund for assistance, because it did not exist. The list is endless.

Possibility includes two dimensions. First, the phenomenon must already exist somewhere in the world system. The phenomenon—be it nuclear weapons, telecommunications satellites, Protestantism, Marxism, or railroads—must have been "invented" so that it is available as a possibility to at least some actors in the system. The second dimension is the distribution of this possibility in the system. Nuclear weapons do exist; however, most states cannot "take advantage" of them because they have neither the wealth nor the expertise to produce their own. The technology needed to place telecommunications satellites in space is known but is not affordable by all. Though a possibility may exist, limits on resources will affect the ability to make use of it.

The unequal distribution of possibilities also makes it *probable* that certain opportunities will be taken. Environmental constraints in any situation make certain behavior more or less likely—there is some normally expected behavior in the situation under consideration. Given that interaction between states is possible, what is the probability they will act in certain ways? For example, what was the probability that the United States and the Soviet Union, the only two superpowers after World War II, would become rivals? Or the probability of interaction between Thailand and Bolivia, small powers in different regions of the world that are separated by thousands of miles? Given the characteristics of the domestic environment (a country's size, wealth, form of government, and ethnic diversity), what is the probability of certain behavior?

To summarize, opportunity requires three related conditions: (1) an international environment that permits interaction between states, (2) states that possess adequate resources to be capable of certain kinds of actions, and (3) decision makers who are aware of both the range of interactions and the extent of capabilities available to them.[3] Opportunity is the possibility of interaction because of objective conditions that may be perceived in varying ways by decision makers.

Willingness

Willingness is concerned with the motivations that lead people to avail themselves of opportunities. Willingness deals with the goals and motivations of decision makers and focuses on why decision makers choose one course over another. Willingness is therefore based on perceptions of the global scene and of domestic political conditions. It derives from calculations of the costs and benefits of alternative courses of action, based not only on objective factors but also on perceptions (for instance, of threat)

---

3. Opportunity can be illustrated with a reference to Lewis Fry Richardson (1960), one of the pioneers of the study of war and peace. Richardson, concerned with "deadly quarrels," drew a parallel between war and murder. Asking why people in one country tended to murder each other more often than they murdered foreigners, he drew the simple conclusion that they had much less opportunity to murder foreigners, since there were far fewer contacts with them. In fact, police records indicate that a person is most likely to be murdered by close relatives or friends, because constant contact and high levels of interaction provide the opportunity for murder. Similar ideas on levels of interaction have been incorporated into simulations of two–level security management by Simon and Starr (1996).

and emotions (for instance, fear, insecurity, or desire for revenge). Willingness thus depends on choice and perception. People react according to what they think they can do and what others expect them to do.

Decision makers behave on the basis of their perception of the world, a perception that may be very different from what the world is actually like. Such differences may be brought home in many ways when the decision maker attempts to implement a policy in the real world. History provides us with the picture of Hitler isolated in his Berlin bunker, moving divisions on a map—lost divisions that were real only to him and that had no impact on the Red Army as it moved inexorably toward the German capital. Thus, when we study different environments, we are also interested in how they affect the image of the world that decision makers hold. Willingness will involve all those factors that affect how decision makers see the world, process information about the world, and make choices.

As noted in the introduction, it is important to understand that *both* opportunity and willingness are required for a given behavior to occur; they are jointly necessary conditions. Wishing for something to happen is not enough—the capabilities to act for its fulfillment must be available. Likewise, simply being able to do something doesn't mean it will happen unless you have the will to take action. Successful deterrence, for example, requires both appropriate weapons—the opportunity—and the willingness to pay the political and military costs of carrying out one's deterrent threat by using the weapons. Indeed, Cioffi-Revilla and Starr (1995, 448) employ opportunity and willingness to distinguish between types of deterrence:

> Credibility is the ability to execute threats (opportunity) and the willingness to do so. In turn, these concepts distinguish and clarify the two types of nuclear deterrence, homeland deterrence and extended deterrence. In analyses of US-Soviet homeland deterrence, willingness is a minor issue and is assumed to exist if the other side initiates a nuclear strike. The key issue in homeland deterrence is the *opportunity* or *ability* to retaliate with credibility; i.e. how to protect weapons, maintain second-strike capability . . . Conversely, extended deterrence focuses mostly on *willingness*—will the aggressor actually attack, will the defender assist the protege?

The Menu

Opportunity, willingness, and the relationships between the decision-making entity and its environment can be summarized and brought together through the analogy of a menu (Russett 1972). The person (entity or actor) who enters a restaurant is confronted by a gastronomical environment—

the menu. The menu provides a number of behavioral opportunities, not determining the diner's choice but constraining what is possible (pizza, lasagna, and linguine are possible in an Italian restaurant, but chicken chow mein and matzo ball soup are not). The menu also affects the probability of the diner's choice through price, portion size, side dishes, specials, and the restaurant's reputation for certain foods. In the Italian restaurant whose reputation rests on its extraordinary pizza, the menu still offers other selections. The probabilities they will be ordered are affected by how the diner sees those choices.

Though the restaurant is not known for its lasagna, which is very expensive, lasagna is still a possibility. A patron who is Chinese and unable to read English (and even is unfamiliar with the Latin alphabet) may order the lasagna, believing that he or she is ordering pizza. A patron who is rich and who is obsessed with lasagna of any quality may also make this selection. Thus, knowledge of a patron's resources and individual decision-making process in relation to the menu, as well as the diner's perception of it, permits us to analyze his or her restaurant behavior. The key to the menu analogy is to understand that the opportunities of international actors are constrained (or enabled) in various ways at various levels of analysis and that these constraints affect the willingness of decision makers to act.

Interdependence and the World System: Conflict and Cooperation

To understand the *international* system and its interdependencies, we must understand the changing menu and the attempts of states to adapt to that menu. As new states and other international actors have come into being and as new technologies and ideologies have altered the international environment, the practices of states and other international actors have adapted to these changes to maintain order within the international system. It is necessary to understand how interdependence *both* contributes to the problems of creating order and creates the conditions necessary for attaining order. Broadly speaking, in this chapter we will look at interdependence and its effects on order; in chapters 3 and 4 we will outline the ways in which international actors attempt to overcome the problems of cooperation and coordination in an anarchic but interdependent world system of externalities and collective goods.

I have stated that interdependence is a quality of all systems and that we can think of world politics as a system. Systems thinking emphasizes wholeness and holistic thinking: looking at the international system means looking at the overall patterns of interactions among the actors. Interdependence emphasizes the links or interconnectedness among the units of a system. Interdependence is one form of constraint that the system places on the state and other actors in terms of opportunities or possibilities and on decision makers in terms of willingness. What is on one actor's menu depends very much on how that menu is connected to the menus of other actors.

How might interdependence constrain the menu? The conception of interdependence used here is based on the notion that changes or events in any single unit of a system will produce some reaction from or have some significant consequence on other units of the system—*whether they like it or not.* The images of the global village, the spaceship earth, and the shrinking planet are all derived from this idea of interdependence and its two different dimensions, sensitivity and vulnerability (Keohane and Nye 1989). In the first place, international actors are *sensitive* to the behavior of other actors or developments in other parts of the system. The degree of sensitivity depends on how quickly change in one actor brings about changes in another and how great the effects are. Second, actors may be *vulnerable* to the effects of those changes. Vulnerability is measured by the costs imposed on a state or other actor by external events, even if that actor tries to avoid those costs in responding to those effects.

A state is sensitive to environmental interdependence if it has to clean beaches blackened by an oil spill that occurred in another state's territorial waters or if a downstream state like the Netherlands must suffer from the river pollution produced by states farther upstream on the Rhine. Such a state is then vulnerable because even after the cleanup, its environment may remain impaired and the effects of the damage may be great, perhaps affecting its tourist and fishing industries. In discussing economic interdependence, we may say that if Japan's trade with the United States drops as a result of a recession in America, that trade is sensitive; if Japan also goes into a recession because of the trade drop, it is vulnerable.[4]

Thus, different systems, and different actors within those systems, may be characterized by different levels of sensitivity and vulnerability. If sensitivity reflects the speed and effects of changes in one part of the system on other parts, then the current system that encompasses the globe and is linked together with modern communication and transportation networks is more highly sensitive than in past eras of international relations. Technology affects the international system by affecting the oppor-

---

4. The United States is certainly not as vulnerable to a recession in, say, Guatemala, as Guatemala is to a U.S. recession. Guatemala may be dependent on the United States, but the two are not interdependent (with *mutual* sensitivities and vulnerabilities at least on this issue) as we have defined the term.

tunities available and by affecting the strength of the interdependent ties among the system's component actors.

One view of interdependence is *positive and optimistic,* seeing interdependence as leading toward more and more cooperation among states as they are brought together. The models of integration, which will become important later, are based on increasing the linkages of interdependence through functional integration (as in the movement for European unity) or through social, economic, and political integration based on transactions. Some integration models go so far as to predict that the outcomes of these integration processes will eventually lead to world community or a world state.

Another view, however, points to interdependence as a constraint on states and therefore as a potentially very important source of conflict. Interdependences—generated *outside* the sovereign state but imposing externalities upon it—can also generate frustration and anger, as states hopelessly wish for past times when they were not inextricably linked with others and when they had greater freedom of action. Mutual dependence need not mean mutual reward (as is required in integration), but potentially mutual harm. Or, in the words of Oran Young (1980), "the growth of interdependence increases the capacity of all relevant actors to injure each other."

Interdependence challenges key elements of sovereignty—independence of action, control over internal affairs, consent in international interaction. In a Realist world, where security is the central issue and military might the primary measure of power, conflicts generated by interdependence may be addressed (usually ineffectually) through force and coercion. Vulnerability can cause military conflict if a state finds it impossible to prevent others from imposing costs on it: U.S. interests in assuring relatively cheap oil, for example, contributed to American use of the military to oppose Iraq. Population growth in one part of the world or greater demand in another can also affect others by the consumption of nonrenewable resources. The consumption of food that others need or the production of pollution that fouls air or kills fish in the waters of other states will affect vulnerable states whether they want to be affected or not.

Interdependence and the idea of sovereignty, which carries the formal and legal assumption of autonomy and equality among states, *do not mix well.* Look again at the Peace of Westphalia. The statesmen and leaders who fashioned this settlement were creating agreements that met the needs of that time. Very clear *trade-offs* were made between autonomy and self-control on the one hand and the lack of order inherent in the anarchic international system on the other: princes who were striving for independence of action from the control of religious or imperial authority (the

Pope and the Holy Roman Emperor) were willing to create a system of states that had no formal source of authority or higher order. This trade-off, sensible at the time, has fostered a set of contemporary problems arising from growth in the levels and scope of interdependence.

The "Westphalian trade-off" stressed independence and autonomy; interdependence stresses collective problems and solutions. The balance has been changing, especially in the decades since World War II. In this period the trade-off has come to stress the need to reduce the formal anarchy of the system in order to solve the problems of interdependence. International law, created as a way to provide some degree of order among states, recognized that sovereignty was based on the autonomy of those states. International law, therefore, attempted to create order among states through the idea of *consent,* or self-constraint. How does interdependence produce constraints without consent? The answer derives from the elements of sensitivity and vulnerability. Interdependence can cause conflict if a sensitive state does not wish to be sensitive; for example, many trading countries were greatly affected in 1971, when the United States surprised the world by devaluing the dollar.

A sensitive state need not be a vulnerable one, however. Larger, wealthier, more powerful states may be able to deal with their sensitivities. Thus, asymmetric levels of sensitivity and vulnerability (especially) can also create "pathologies of interdependence." These pathologies can be seen in the theories of international political economy that deal with unequal exchange (e.g,. see Caporaso 1993). These theories include the various models of dependency developed from a radical or Neo-Marxist perspective. Looking at the world from the perspective of developing, non-Western countries, interdependence is often seen as bringing back the dominance and exploitation of former colonial periods.

A "New" Interdependence?

Some analysts focus on the extensive new webs of interdependence that are creating a truly global system for the first time. Through technology and the dismantling of colonial empires, there is much that is new; however, much of what is being seen as interdependence is not new but is just being recognized for the first time. Thus, we can talk about both the *conditions* of interdependence (the existence of linkages that hold the system together) and the *cognitions* of interdependence (people seeing or perceiving that interdependence exists).

Many of today's conditions are indeed quite new, especially in that some states are much more sensitive and vulnerable than ever before. The world system is populated by a large number of states that are small and poor and have only a token degree of autonomy. Many of these states are constantly buffeted by systemic economic, monetary, and political forces and are far more sensitive and vulnerable than most states in the past have been. They, and all international actors, are more interdependent because of the increasing opportunities for interaction that have been provided by technological advances in communication and transportation—the increasing ability to send words and things farther, faster, and at less cost. Rosenau (1990, esp. chaps.12, 13) has argued that this "microelectronic revolution" is one of the five major sources of change transforming the basic parameters of the global system, being

> . . . the shift from an industrial to a postindustrial order [that] focuses on the dynamics of technology, particularly on those technologies associated with the microelectronic revolution that have made social, economic, and political distances much shorter, the movement of ideas, pictures, currencies, and information so much faster, and thus the interdependence of people and events so much greater. (12)

Increasing linkages have occurred not only between governmental elites, but also through and across all segments of the population of a state, often facilitated by the activities of nongovernmental organizations (NGOs) such as multinational corporations. These linkages have been discussed for a quarter century in the literature on transnational relations, globalism, and regimes. While following in the transnationalist tradition, Rosenau stresses in his analysis of the microelectronic revolution that in today's world, many of these linkages can now occur with an incredible speed that was missing in earlier periods.[5]

Technology has expanded not only the physical capabilities of people to interact with each other, but also consciousness of that interaction. To Rosenau (1990, 88), a major consequence of the microelectronic revolution is the rapid spread throughout the world of analytic capabilities to individual citizens: "those predispositions and practices by which people relate to higher authority, a cluster that includes their loyalties, legitimacy sentiments, compliance habits, analytic skills, and cathectic capacities." It is important to note that if one combines the increased number and kinds of linkages—or *transactions*–cutting across state boundaries, at all levels of society, and involving all manner of individual and group actors, with

---

5. As noted in Starr (1991b, 925), Rosenau's *Turbulence,* "while going beyond transnational relations and complex interdependence approaches with its model of postinternational politics, clearly emerges from the transnational relations (and integration studies) tradition. . . ."

these notions of loyalty or legitimacy or compliance, one arrives at the core of the Deutschian social communication model of integration!

These analytic capabilities of individuals come from increased computer usage and the ability to communicate through telephone networks, electronic mail and fax facilities, and radio and television. Rosenau notes that the number of television transmitters in the world increased more than sevenfold from 1965 to 1985 (from 8,500 to over 60,000); television sets worldwide rose from 186 million in 1965 to 661 million in 1985. Thus, the "new" interdependence is based to a large degree on new patterns of human attention. Individuals can see things that are happening in faraway places, anywhere on the planet. The democratic revolutions across Eastern Europe have been called the "television revolutions," as people in each country watched and then emulated what had just happened somewhere else in the region.

The microelectronic revolution highlights the psychological dimension of interdependence. This psychological aspect means that people are not only aware that activities are taking place elsewhere, but they are aware that they are aware. They understand that they belong to some sort of global village, to use Marshall McLuhan's famous term, and that they exist in some larger world system. Television and radio have brought foreign events—"live and in color"—into homes all around the world: "For Shakespeare it was a metaphor, but for our generation it has become a reality: the world is now literally a stage, as its actors dance across the TV screen" (Rosenau 1990, 344).

The amount and degree of interdependence in the international system thus depend on a number of factors, such as the technology of communications and transportation. These factors affect the number and the types of interaction that occur between and among international actors, how resources and capabilities are distributed within the system, and how vulnerable single states and other actors are. Interdependence increases as states become more vulnerable to penetration of various kinds. Interdependence can occur only when the hard shell of the state—its sovereignty—is cracked.

Because of both increased interdependence and increased awareness of interdependence, governmental decision makers have to think about and take into account the effects their *internal* policies have on foreign relations with other states—for example, U.S. economic choices dealing with the size of its national debt and governmental deficit, South African treatment of its black population through most of the post–World War II period, or Israeli treatment of its Arab citizens. The remarkable changes in South African politics and the progress toward peace by Israel and its neighbors were clearly impelled by interdependence in a post–cold war era. There is no doubt that whether actions, events, or policies were meant to cross state boundaries or to affect the peoples and governments of other states, they do. That, in a nutshell, is interdependence.

Transnational Relations and Interdependence

In an era of increasing interdependences, national boundaries have become less and less relevant (as will be discussed further in chapter 5). Many scholars, writers, and even diplomats feel that continuing to view the world in terms of the traditional Westphalian logic is not very useful and may be downright harmful, given the nature of contemporary interdependences. These observers are implicitly calling for a reversal of the Westphalian trade–off; they feel that if governments continue to look at the world in terms of old (Realist) images (including that of sovereign nation-states concerned with independent behavior and military power), such views will lead to wrongheaded policies that may have disastrous consequences. This view has been extensively expressed by scholars who see the world in terms of transnational relations rather than international relations.

Transnationalism has been described as the movement of goods, information, and ideas across national boundaries without significant, direct participation or control by high-level governmental actors: "A good deal of intersocietal intercourse, with significant political importance, takes place without governmental control" (Nye and Keohane 1971, 330). These patterns of penetration and linkage involve heavy participation by various kinds of nonstate actors, particularly NGOs.[6] This transnational view clearly reduces the importance of the ideas of sovereignty, national boundaries, and the interaction of governments in the world system. Because each state has become so permeable, so open to outside influences, domestic and international politics have become indistinguishable. This blurring of the domestic and international, as developed later, is a significant challenge to several assumptions of Realism.

The main point to note is the multiplicity of interactions that bypass the governments of states and act directly on their domestic environments. In the transnational view, nonstate actors (NGOs in particular) are much more important actors than previously thought, as are the interest groups or subnational actors that exist within states. A growing literature now dis-

---

6. For example, Nye and Keohane (1971, 331) note an interest "in a wide variety of transnational phenomena: multinational business enterprises and revolutionary movements; trade unions and scientific networks [presaging Peter Haas's concept of "epistemic communities"]; international air transport cartels and communications activities in outer space." See also the volume of collected papers on transnational relations in Keohane and Nye 1972.

cusses the influence of tribal, ethnic, or separatist groups within states—as well as older literature that looks at economic interests, multinational corporations (MNCs), and parts of the governmental bureaucracy. These last factors, acting in accordance with the organizational process model, often interact directly with comparable parts of other states' bureaucracies, many times without the knowledge of the top decision makers of the states involved. As discussed by Huntington (1973) and Keohane and Nye (1974), such "transgovernmental" relations could be consistent with Haasian neofunctional processes of integration as well.

Both NGOs and the subnational actors are distinct from state actors and can act independently from states. These transnational actors make up Rosenau's "multicentric" world—the groups of many thousands of diverse actors (individuals, groups, organizations, movements)—that seek autonomy of action *from* states. According to Rosenau, in the multicentric world of non-sovereignty-bound, nonstate (and nonterritorial) actors, the key issue is the "autonomy dilemma" of freedom of action rather than the "security dilemma" of states.

The transnational view holds that nonstate actors can affect nation-states. Power and influence are a result of the relations between actors. The different needs and vulnerabilities of states, international governmental organizations (IGOs), and NGOs provide all actors with some levers of influence in their dealings with other actors. Here, "power" takes on forms that are not considered in Realist analyses. For example, Ward and House (1988) present a provocative view of "behavioral power" that permits entities normally seen as "weak" to exert significant influence in world politics. They can do so because, even though "small" by such Realist standards of power as military capability, they are able to have an impact on the sensitivity and vulnerability of other actors through the dynamics of interdependence. That is, through interdependence, Ward and House provide a "robust mechanism for examining the multilateral interactions of nations in the international system . . . [providing] a unique and potentially useful addition to classic capability-based approaches to measuring power" (Ward and House 1988, 31).

Indeed, interdependence generates a new set of problems and demands on those in authority. In Realist models, the power of states has been conceived as, and based primarily upon, military capability. But numerous analysts (e.g., Baldwin 1989) have shown that military capability is not easily convertible across issue areas and situations. Such analysts have argued that military capability is *not fungible;* it is not interchangeable with other mechanisms of influence and cannot easily be substituted for other mechanisms or converted into other elements of influence. Thus, states that base their "power" on military capabilities are not necessarily well equipped to handle the demands (vulnerabilities and sensitivities) of transnational interdependence.[7]

In sum, the Westphalian, state-centered view focuses on power and security and is, in essence, the Realist view of international politics. In the transnational view, such matters are no longer central but are replaced by economic, cultural, social, and other concerns. As with the phenomenon of integration, a transnational perspective presents us with a multitude of anomalies, things that we should not expect to happen (or to be important) if the Realist view of the world were to hold.

> For every quintessential "realist" happening—such as the Soviet invasion of Afghanistan or the U.S. intervention in Central America—innumerable events occur for which realism has, at best, a strained and insufficient explanation. A private group, the Natural Resources Defense Council (NRDC), negotiates with the superpower governments to monitor nuclear test-ban agreements; a representative of the Church of England serves as a link between terrorists and governments in the Middle East; a variety of organizations make decisions to invest or disinvest in an effort to alter the social policies of the South African government; the IMF instructs national governments on their economic policies; . . . Poles in the United States are given the franchise in the 1989 Polish elections, and their ballots are believed to be decisive in one Warsaw district; . . . a novel published in England leads to the withdrawal of ambassadors from Iran and to an assassination in Belgium; two poisoned grapes from Chile disrupt world markets, provoke actions by several governments, lead to labor tensions in the docks of Philadelphia, and foster disarray in Chile itself. (Rosenau 1990, 93–94)

Clearly, removing military issues from the center of the issue agenda is based on the increasing sensitivity and vulnerability of states and non-state actors to *economic* interdependencies. International economic relationships are becoming more and more sensitive to domestic economic factors such as taxation, inflation, and monetary policy. The reverse is also true. U.S. relations with European allies, the strength of the dollar on world money markets, and thus the economic standing of the United States—as well as its trade policies regarding arms, technology, and food—are all related to domestic policies on deficits and a balanced bud-

---

7. Rosenau (1990) has called this phenomenon "the narrowing competence of governments" and has contrasted the influence and freedom of "sovereignty-bound" actors within the statecentric world to the "sovereignty-free" actors of the multicentric world. Much of Rosenau's chapter 2 reinforces Ward and House's 1988 concept of "behavioral power."

get. Advocates of the transnational view want to highlight the relationships between international politics and international economics. According to a transnational perspective, domestic politics can influence international economics directly, and vice versa, and domestic economics can affect international politics directly, and vice versa.[8]

One of the main instruments by which economic interdependences have increased is the MNC. MNCs are just one of the postwar challenges to the nation–state. The global "megacorporation" is transforming the world political economy through its increasing control over three fundamental resources of economic life: the technology of production, finance capital, and marketing (Barnet and Cavanaugh 1994). As Gilpin (1987, 260–61) notes, while capital and technology have become more and more mobile, labor, relatively, has not. Industry is no longer constrained by geography, since production makes national boundaries irrelevant—the more important factors for the location of production facilities are those that create incentives such as tax breaks, low-cost labor, and nearness to markets.

Transnational production also makes loyalty to any one state irrelevant. As examples of Rosenau's non-sovereignty-bound actors, such corporations have become "less and less accountable." Although loyalty is the basis of nationalism, MNCs are careful not to favor any country in which they do business over any other such country.[9] Gilpin (1987, 261) notes simply that, "The result of this internationalization of industrial production has been the creation of a complex web of interlocking relationships among nation-states and the world's giant corporations." We will return to the question of commerce and borders, economics and sovereignty, the state and nonstate actors in chapter 5.[10]

---

8. It may be possible to connect Realism to economics in similar ways, but as Caporaso (1993, 465) argues, while Realism is not incapable in principle, "realism will have to break new ground" to do so. Caporaso (1993, 461) outlines the problem: "Given the interest in explaining war and peace, realism does not have to take on the additional burden of explaining variations in national power. Yet, to connect to economics, realism must move beyond security issues narrowly defined." He suggests several ways in which the realist concern for power can be linked to economic exchange and institutions.

9. Rosenau (1990, 255) notes: "A particularly incisive indicator of the autonomy that has accrued to actors in the multi-centric world is the readiness of U.S. companies to abandon their national identity and proclaim themselves global enterprises whose well-being is no longer dependent on the American economy."

10. Although economically oriented, transnationalism does include nonstate transnational actors that are concerned with military activity, such as guerrilla movements and terrorist groups. These groups may be seen as transnational actors, penetrating the state's hard shell; their activity may also lead to governmental interactions and thus to more interdependence in the system. Much more can be said about terrorism as a transnational phenomenon, but that is not the purpose of this chapter.

The growth of transnational interactions and interdependences in the post–World War II era has helped produce new problems and new challenges to the state; the environment has changed, and international actors have faced the problem of adaptation. Together, these new conditions and the problems they have engendered mirror the transnationalist perspective's challenge to Realism. This challenge, and the foregoing discussion, can be summarized in the three elements of Keohane and Nye's 1989 concept of "complex interdependence": (1) complex interdependence refutes the notion that only states count and argues that there are numerous other consequential actors and interactions; (2) complex interdependence argues that there no longer exists a set hierarchy of issues dominated by the concerns of military security; and (3) the arguments of complex interdependence preclude the use of military force among a number of states.

The freedom and independence promised by sovereignty have been buffeted and confronted by technology, economics, and nonstate actors that regularly penetrate the state's hard shell. This period has been one of turbulence, characterized both by high levels of complexity and by high degrees of change. Rosenau calls this period of transition, when long-term patterns of behavior are in flux, "postinternational politics." We can characterize it as yet another way of indicating a shift in the Westphalian trade-off, as states seek to adapt to a changing environment. *And in so doing,* they are attempting to cope with the central question of this book: How to manage interdependence?

How interdependence and externalities create new issues, needs, and problems—and how states can adapt to deal with these new conditions—is addressed next in chapter 3. In Part 2, we will expand on many of the points raised in the next chapter.

CHAPTER 3

Interdependence and Collective Goods: Interests and Order for Individuals and Groups

Individuals, Groups, and Interdependence

The last chapter introduced interdependence as the initial building block for the approach to world order presented in this book. It is not enough, however, to say simply that interdependence exists and is therefore important. We are concerned with "how to manage interdependence" *because* of the consequences of interdependence for the interdependent units. The implications of interdependence for opportunity and willingness, adaptation, and order in the international system must be drawn and extended. That is the purpose of the present chapter.

States act to achieve their goals and interests both singly and in groups. As the world has become more tightly linked through various interdependences, states have found themselves grouped together in international organizations and regional groupings or subsystems that are economic, political, and military in nature. States also belong to a world system. We may think of each state (as well as the other international actors) as a member of a group (or system) that includes the entire globe. Being a member of a group complicates what any individual member can achieve and how the member achieves it because of the working of the sensitivity and vulnerability of interdependence. Clearly, interdependence affects how individual interests relate to group interests. Sometimes state policymakers think they are acting in their own interests when they are not. This is yet another argument for transnationalism; it points out that the traditional notion of individual states seeking their own special or national interests is now counterproductive in a world where states are enmeshed in many different kinds of groups.

If individuals are in some way "rational"—that is, minimally purposeful in the connecting of ends and means—how can policymakers not act in their own best interests? The key to this question is yet another aspect of the entity-environment relationship: how individual interests

27

relate to group interests; how the interests and menu of any single entity relate to the context of the interests and menus of the group(s) within which it is embedded. As we know, these concerns are found in the Prisoner's Dilemma—the temptation to maximize individual payoffs against the best outcome that the "group" (the two prisoners) can achieve. In many ways the Prisoner's Dilemma is central to the Realist argument joining systemic anarchy to self-help and the security dilemma. However, Realist analyses minimize or ignore the degree to which the relationship between individual and group interests is based on interdependence, externalities, and the degree to which any good can be conceived of as a "collective good."

While collective goods have been treated at length, and in complex, technical detail by economists, sociologists, and political scientists, the individual-group relationship may be clearly and simply illustrated using a passage from *Catch-22,* Joseph Heller's classic novel set during World War II. Yossarian, a bombardier in the U.S. Army Air Force in Italy, refuses to fly any more missions. Major Major, a superior officer, in trying to persuade Yossarian to fly, asks, "Would you like to see our country lose?" Yossarian replies, "We won't lose. We've got more men, more money and more material. There are ten million men in uniform getting killed and a lot more are making money and having fun. Let somebody else get killed." Major Major replies, "But suppose everybody on our side felt that way." Yossarian's answer is devastatingly to the point: "Then I'd certainly be a damn fool to feel any other way. Wouldn't I?" (Heller 1961, 107).

This episode raises the central dilemma of the individual and the group: the interdependence of units within a system. If all the other fliers are willing to fly their missions, then Yossarian would be a fool to go along, because with ten million men in the war, his individual presence will not make a difference. On the other hand, if none of the others wishes to fly either, then his response, "I'd be a damned fool to feel any other way," is a rational answer. His presence would again make no difference. However, if all the other fliers were to take the same position, then the following version of the Prisoner's Dilemma develops: despite the fact that missions have to be flown, it is not rational for any single individual to participate. That is, it is not rational for any individual player to cooperate when the other player(s) defect—the classic "sucker" payoff in the Prisoner's Dilemma. Each player is tempted to defect, defection being the strategy that promises the least individual loss (and possibly the greatest individual gain) in a Prisoner's Dilemma situation.[1]

---

1. It is useful to recall at this point that the Prisoner's Dilemma is the name for a social situation that occurs in many different areas of human interaction—a situation with a special

For the collective—a group of individuals—the goal of winning the war can be achieved only through group action. Yet such group action consists of the activities of individuals, and Yossarian makes it clear that it does not seem rational for any single individual to perform the actions needed to achieve the group's goal. So, how do groups of supposedly rational actors ever accomplish group or collective goals? Why, for example, should any single state stop hunting whales, stop polluting the oceans or the air, stop increasing population, stop increasing its use of oil, obey international law, or participate in arms control?

The dilemma rests in large part in the nature of the goods being provided, seeing "goods" as economists do, to imply simply the consequences of an activity. If such outcomes, consequences, or payoffs are tangible things that can be possessed as property by a single person, they are what economists call *private goods*. A private good is fully or perfectly divisible, and it is "appropriable"—that is, it can be split up, and parts can be used or consumed by individual members of a group. The consumption of a private good by one person reduces the amount of that good left for any other individual.

---

set of incentives for choice. It belongs to a class of situations (or games) called "variable sum" or "mixed motive," as opposed to the zero–sum situation, which characterizes much of Realist analysis. Zero-sum situations are those in which whatever one player wins, the other must lose. In variable-sum situations such as the Prisoner's Dilemma, both players may win, both may lose, or one may win while the other loses.

The dilemma occurs in the tension between trust and temptation, in the tension between individual and group interests (the interest of both players collectively). A typical Prisoner's Dilemma matrix, such as that presented here, indicates two players who have the choice either to cooperate with each other or to defect from the other. The payoffs of the Prisoner's Dilemma create the following incentive structure: $T > R > P > S$. This means that the best payoff comes from the *T*emptation to defect while the other player cooperates; the second-best payoff is from the *R*ewards of mutual cooperation; the third-best payoff is from the *P*unishment of mutual defection; but the *worst* outcome is being caught as the *S*ucker—cooperating while the other defects.

Thus, while the group (both players collectively) does best when both players cooperate (*R,R* in the following matrix), the incentives for a rational player lead the player to defect (*T*)—either as protection from the other player's defection (to avoid *S*) or as an aggressive attempt to catch the other as a sucker. Since both players make the same calculation, the incentive structure of the situation drives them to double defection (*P,P*) whereas they would best serve the group interests by cooperating (*R,R*).

	Player Alpha	
Player Beta	Cooperate	Defect
Cooperate	3,3 (*R,R*)	1,4 (*S,T*)
Defect	4,1 (*T,S*)	2,2 (*P,P*)

Source: Russett and Starr 1992, 306.

The "central metaphor" of economics is "allocation" (Caporaso and Levine 1992, 22). Private goods form the basis of most of the analysis involved in the study of economics. Economists have been concerned with how private goods are distributed, or allocated, among people. The allocation of private goods involves questions of costs, of how people value things. Costs are determined by supply and demand: how much is available and how much of the good people want. Economists study how supply and demand, influenced by the market mechanism, determine the prices of things and their distribution. Under ideal conditions, private goods and the market solve the individual-group problem pointed out by Yossarian: each individual, seeking to maximize his or her own interests, buys and sells as desired, affected only by supply and demand. If each individual seeks to do so in an economic system where only private goods exist, the whole group will benefit if each person follows individual interests.

Thus, with private goods we can achieve the "ideal" condition of Pareto optimality—a condition of distribution where the group (or society) has essentially maximized the relationship of the individual and the group. At Pareto optimality it is impossible to make any single member better off without making someone else worse off. With private goods, the free market works *because* of the maximizing rationality of each individual involved in the market. If *each* individual attempts to gain the greatest benefit at the least cost, in a world where the things they value have the properties of private goods, and there is a perfectly working market, then the individual-group dilemma is solved: while each person "rationally" attempts to maximize individual gain, the whole group itself will benefit.

Let us return to Yossarian's (actually Major Major's) dilemma. Suppose there existed a world consisting *only* of private goods, not in winning a war or preserving democracy. Then individuals would fly in combat only if they would receive something that they could possess as a private good, like money. Pilots would fly if someone paid them enough, and the market mechanism would work to get some people to fly. If an insufficient number of pilots came forward, the pay for flying would increase, and more people would be willing to fly. But as the supply of fliers increased, the pay would go down, and fewer people would come forward; eventually there would be a fairly stable number of pilots willing to fly bombers. The whole group benefits from this situation.

But any (even casual) observer knows that the world doesn't work this way. The market mechanism based on supply and demand does not, in fact, work perfectly; it works poorly for many goods and not at all for others. This reality is the phenomenon of "market failure," the analysis of which permeates most contemporary analyses of economic relations.[2] For many goods, the allocation of scarce resources—based on how costs and benefits affect the choices of individuals—derives from considerations other than supply and demand. Many goods have properties and characteristics that make them different from private goods. These are goods that have "externalities." Externalities affect people's choices, costs, and benefits through factors other than supply and demand.

Without externalities, one's costs and benefits derive from one's own values and desires, and the cost of goods is determined by the producer (his or her own costs, profit margin, and so on). If externalities are present, however, the activities of other consumers and producers can affect both one's benefits and the producer's costs. For example, Jones buys a cat for the private good of killing the mice on his property. However, those mice also bothered Smith's property, so that by eating the mice, Jones's cat has produced benefits for Smith: an externality. During the nineteenth century, to protect its private good of security for its colonial possessions and its profitable trade, the British navy policed the sea lanes to the Western Hemisphere and prevented possible intervention by other European major powers. Like Jones's cat, the British navy provided externalities to the young United States, which also benefited from the conditions for secure trade.

Externalities can also increase costs. For example, Jones's new car, while a private good in the sense that it belongs to him and only he can ride in it, is also bright red. Smith, whose front window directly overlooks Jones's driveway, becomes sick at the sight of bright red. Smith thus incurs costs from Jones's car: she can look out her window and get sick or keep the curtains drawn and not be able to see outside—and have to use more electricity for lighting instead of natural light. Citing a real-case scenario, the Soviet Union made a private decision to provide its own electricity through nuclear power. In 1986 one of its "private" nuclear plants at Chernobyl had an accident, and all its European neighbors to the west also incurred the costs of being exposed to radiation and in cleaning up that radiation.

As with interdependence in general, the consequences of externalities can be any combination of positive and negative effects. Externalities involve the spillover of effects to other members of the group (or other units in the system), and changes or activities in one unit produce effects in another: sensitivities and vulnerabilities! Just as with interdependence,

---

2. I offer just two examples. First, in his state-of-the-discipline overview of "global political economy," one of the first topics that Caporaso (1993, 452–57) addresses is "Market Failure: Externalities and Public Goods." Second, Keohane's 1984 discussion of the need for regimes (chap. 6) begins with the consideration of imperfect markets and market failures.

externalities can generate conflict if they produce harmful effects, and interdependently connected units cannot escape their vulnerabilities (the "forced rider" noted subsequently). Thus, just as with interdependence, sovereignty does not mix well with externalities and may result in conflict if the effects are negative: "The principle of sovereignty in effect establishes rules of liability that put the burden of externalities on those *who suffer from them*" (Keohane 1984, 8, emphasis added).

Characteristics of Collective Goods

Collective goods are goods with certain kinds of externality properties. Here the externalities are found in their most extreme form; the existence of collective goods thus also implies a system connected by powerful bonds of interdependence. Collective goods possess two special characteristics, the first a prerequisite for the second. More important, these two characteristics describe a "pure" collective good, something rarely found in the real world. For that reason we should think of goods as being more or less characterized by collective-good properties.

The first special characteristic, perhaps the key one, is *jointness of supply.* If a good is supplied to any member of a group, then it is supplied to all members of that group. Jointness of supply also means that if new members are added to the group, the other members who also consume the good will not receive a diminished amount. Thus, in clear distinction from private goods, collective goods are indivisible. The classic example is that of a lighthouse—if it shines its light to guide one ship, then all other ships in that area (the group) can also use the lighthouse. Additional ships, moreover, will not diminish the amount of the good provided (so long as one ship does not physically impede another). When a government provides deterrence for its population, that deterrence is jointly supplied. When Washington threatened Moscow with retaliation for an attack on the United States, it provided deterrence for every individual in the United States. Once one person is protected by the deterrent threat, all are protected; once California is protected, so are Montana and Delaware. An increase in population does not reduce the deterrence provided to all the rest. The addition of Alaska and Hawaii in 1959 did not diminish the deterrence already being provided to the other forty-eight states.

Again, goods are the consequences of activities and are not necessarily positive. A factory that produces pollution in an area is producing a jointly supplied "good." The pollution that any one individual breathes can be consumed by all other individuals in an area. Again, more people in the area will not take away from the pollution available to the others. Any form of air or water pollution, then, is a jointly supplied good. Similarly, clean air provided by pollution controls and government programs is also a jointly supplied good, whether in the domestic or the international arena.

The second characteristic of an ideal collective good is called *nonexclusiveness*. A jointly supplied good may be either excludable or nonexcludable; that is, even though it is jointly supplied, it can be withheld from nonmembers. Cable television is a good example of a jointly supplied good that is excludable. Once the cable signal is supplied to any one cable subscriber, the addition of new subscribers does not reduce the supply of the good. However, it is excludable: those who do not pay for the service are not hooked up to the cable and thus cannot receive the service. Jointly supplied goods, then, can be perfectly excludable. The beam of light from a lighthouse, on the other hand, is a nonexcludable, jointly supplied good. However, if that lighthouse is altered to use a radar signal rather than a light, then the use of the lighthouse can be regulated. All those who do not buy the equipment to receive radar signals would be excluded. The pure collective good, then, is jointly supplied and cannot be controlled for exclusion. If the United States is deterring a nuclear attack on its own territory, it would be physically impossible to exclude any specific group of persons—foreign diplomats or tourists, prisoners, or citizens who do not pay taxes. Any people on the territory of the United States are part of the group included in nuclear deterrence and cannot be excluded from it.

Given the concern here with the entity-environment relationship and the effects of interdependence on conflict and cooperation, there then is a third important aspect of collective goods. It concerns not whether the group providing the good can exclude others, but whether some individual entity can choose whether or not to consume or be affected by the good. We are back to the idea of vulnerability in interdependence and how it might generate conflict. Although someone can choose whether to use a toll road (a jointly supplied good, for the most part) or subscribe to cable TV, that individual cannot choose whether or not to be affected by pollution or an epidemic, or even the military draft or taxes (both somewhat imperfect means of providing collective goods). This is what Sandler, Loehr, and Cauley (1978) call the "forced-rider" problem: individuals being forced to consume the collective good, whether they want to or not and whether or not it has negative effects (externalities) on them. The negative effects of collective goods will generate conflict. International actors are thus faced with managing interdependence and the conflict that interdependence can generate through collective goods. This need to manage interdependence is especially true if we understand that the greater the degree of interdependence in a system, the higher will be the proportion of activities characterized by collective goods.

The Free-Rider Dilemma

These properties of collective goods have important implications for how individuals behave in groups. Winning a war may be seen as a good that has some collective properties. If the war is won, all citizens of the country that wins will have won: some of the benefits—political freedom and ideological victory—will go to all if they go to one. It is also difficult to exclude citizens from this good of winning. Because of that, individuals are faced with the "free-rider" decision: to help in achieving the good or to be a free rider on the efforts of others; (in the parlance of the Prisoner's Dilemma, to cooperate or to defect, respectively). This is exactly the logic that Yossarian used and the dilemma posed by that logic—if everyone wants to be a free rider, the collective good may never be achieved.

In the ideal case, then, where only private goods exist, an economic mechanism—the free market—can allocate goods within a group or society. This mechanism does not work well for the allocation of collective goods because of their indivisibility and nonexcludability. If individuals are strictly rational in the economic sense of desiring to maximize benefits and minimize costs, a collective good may never be provided, even if all members of a group desire that good. This dilemma arises from the clash between individual interests and benefits and group interests and benefits. If the good is a collective good (and thus jointly supplied), the group member will receive its benefits whether that member pays for it or does not (gets a free ride). The rational individual will not have to pay (incur costs) for a benefit that he or she will gain anyway if others pay. The rational individual thus will not pay and will wait for someone else to pay. In addition, one does not want to be the sucker or patsy (in exactly the same sense as being the sucker in the Prisoner's Dilemma) and buy the good that others will enjoy at no cost. That is why Yossarian did not want to be one of those getting killed while others were making money and having fun, not when there were ten million other men in uniform.

The paradox, or irony, is clear. The *same* maximizing rationality for individuals that is essential to the successful working of a free market dealing with private goods, which is essential to approximating the successful equilibrium of individual and group interests, *does not work with collective goods.* In fact, such individual maximizing self-interest can make things worse for everyone! The "invisible hand"—whether in the form of the Realist's balance of power or the Liberal's laissez-faire free market—is inadequate. Economic mechanisms alone will not work to solve the free-rider problem—political and social mechanisms are required. Taylor and Singleton (1993, 66) succinctly summarize a vast literature in political science and economics regarding collective action problems: "The importance of collective action problems in the study of politics cannot be over-estimated. They are *foundational:* were it not for collective action problems *there would be no need for politics*" (emphasis added). The political nature of collective goods is inseparable from their economic nature.

This dilemma is interesting because it shows the extreme interdependence of group members involved with collective goods. If everyone takes a free ride, an important good may not be produced. There can be no arms stability if everyone decides to cheat on arms control. If many decide to take a free ride, a good may be only partially provided, as, for example, when some states refuse to pay dues to international organizations that for various reasons do not wish to throw nonpayers out of the organization. If member states refuse to contribute to the military capabilities of their alliance, alliance security will be underprovided. One major area of research has focused on the extent to which the security (deterrence as opposed to actual defense) provided by an alliance is a collective good. Because alliances can provide some amount of deterrence that has collective-good properties for alliance members (although much less so than in the case of deterrence covering a single country, as noted earlier), alliance burden sharing has been studied in terms of free riding.[3]

In the contemporary world system, more and more objectives of states require group action because of interdependence: ecological challenges, economic issues such as monetary policy and trade, more traditional security issues such as arms control or the nonproliferation of weapons. Perhaps most important, the idea of *order* in the international system itself may be seen as having collective-good properties. If there is some stability, predictability, and regularity in international affairs, adding new actors may not diminish it, and it is difficult (although not impossible) to exclude actors from the benefits of international order and coordination (e.g., Snidal 1985; Oye 1986).

It is possible to interpret the post–Gulf War "new international order" as something from which all members of the group—the world—might benefit. It is an externality, the increase or decrease of which will affect all entities, both state and nonstate. The Gulf War itself may be seen as a warning that the superpower-led United Nations will not tolerate free riders for the collective good of order. Part of the strong reaction to the Iraqi invasion of Kuwait may have stemmed from the perception that it threatened a new chance at order presented by the end of the cold war and that Iraq's behavior adversely affected not just Kuwait, but also the collective good of order for the whole system.

---

3. For a useful overview of this application of collective goods to the analysis of alliance burden sharing, see Sandler 1993 and Thies 1987. The pioneering statement is found in Olson and Zeckhauser 1966.

The desire to develop economically also can be implemented only through group action, such as aid or special trade policies. Many areas of international political economy have been studied using collective goods concepts, including international common property resources like the high seas, international trade, international monetary policy, the creation of international law, and international organizations. The desire to clean up an international body of water like the Rhine or the Mediterranean or to clean up the air also can be achieved only through group action. Although a free-rider state might appear to be following its own interests, in the long run it is acting against them because the good desired—for example, a clean river—may never be achieved. If a river that flows through many countries requires cleaning up, it may never be cleaned if all the countries wait for the others to do it, hoping to reap the benefits without paying. Because the condition of the river is jointly supplied and nonexcludable, anyone on the river will benefit from clean water (just as all will be harmed by polluted water because of the action of one or more countries). Here, free riding will stop the good of clean water from being achieved, cause it to take much longer to achieve, or cause it to be only partially achieved.

The Tragedy of the Commons

As far back as Aristotle it was understood that pressures existed for people to take advantage of collective goods: "What is common to the greatest number has the least care bestowed upon it. Everyone thinks chiefly of his own, hardly at all of the common interest" (*Politics,* Book II, chap. 3). The best example of this variation of the free rider is what Garrett Hardin (1977a) has called the "tragedy of the commons." Hardin (1977a, 20) borrows his use of *tragedy* from Alfred North Whitehead: "The essence of dramatic tragedy is not unhappiness. It resides in the solemnity of the remorseless working of things."

Here, Hardin describes a pasture, the commons, that belongs to all the members of a group:

> The tragedy of the commons develops in this way. Picture a pasture open to all. It is to be expected that each herdsman will try to keep as many cattle as possible on the commons. Such an arrangement may work reasonably satisfactorily for centuries because tribal wars, poaching, and disease keep the numbers of both man and beast well below the carrying capacity of the land. Finally, however, comes the day of reckoning, that is, the day when the long-desired goal of social stability becomes a reality. At this point, the inherent logic of the commons remorselessly generates tragedy.

As a rational being, each herdsman seeks to maximize his gain. Explicitly or implicitly, more or less consciously, he asks, "What is the utility to me of adding one more animal to my herd?" This utility has one negative and one positive component.

1. The positive component is a function of the increment of one animal. Since the herdsman receives all the proceeds from the sale of the additional animal, the positive utility is nearly +1.

2. The negative component is a function of the additional overgrazing created by one more animal. Since, however, the effects of overgrazing are shared by all the herdsmen, the negative utility for any particular decision-making herdsman is only a fraction of 1.

Adding together the component partial utilities, the rational herdsman concludes that the only sensible course for him to pursue is to add another animal to his herd. And another; and another. . . . But this is the conclusion reached by each and every rational herdsman sharing a commons. Therein is the tragedy. Each man is locked into a system that compels him to increase his herd without limiting a world that is limited. Ruin is the destination toward which all men rush, each pursuing his own best interest in a society that believes in the freedom of the commons. Freedom in a commons brings ruin to all. (Hardin 1977a, 20)

By the definition Hardin employs, the commons is a jointly supplied good in the sense that once provided to any member of the group, all may use it. It is *perceived* as infinite, so that any individual's usage is not perceived to diminish the good for other users. Again, by definition, it is nonexcludable for the members of the group—it is the commons. However, it *is* possible, physically, to exclude users. Thus, the commons has some collective goods characteristics (but should not be seen as approximating a pure collective good). The tragedy of the commons is the other side of the free-rider problem. When there are free riders, some collective good is not provided. In the tragedy of the commons, when individuals follow the logic of (maximizing and short-term) rational self-interest, the result is the destruction of a good with collective characteristics that already exists.

The commons can be seen as a collective good with strong jointness properties as long as usage levels remain low, when the use by an additional member does not reduce the use of others. We can characterize the commons using the same two properties that Elinor Ostrom uses to conceptualize *common-pool resources* (CPRs): (1) a natural or artificially created resource system that is sufficiently large to make it costly (but not impossible) to exclude potential appropriators from using the resource, (2) the good is subject to rivalry, [or] subtractibility (Ostrom 1990, 30; Keohane and Ostrom 1995, 13–14). The tragedy occurs when usage increases so that the good is still nonexcludable (again, by definition it is held in common) but now is no longer indivisible. That is, the good is not really jointly supplied, it is finite or has become finite (for any variety of reasons), and the appropriators (either individually or as a group) do not see or understand the change.

Some may see the problem, but as Aristotle noted, do not feel responsible for their own behavior as part of the problem—Yossarian didn't. Hardin (1977b, 72) has pointed out that a commons often leads people to ignore their responsibilities but not their rights to use or exploit the commons. Hardin (1977b, 66) uses Charles Frankel's definition: "A decision is responsible when the man or group that makes it has to answer for it to those who are directly or indirectly affected by it." It should be clear how interdependence and externalities complicate the issue of responsibility. In the international arena, questions of responsibility have been even more problematic, because sovereignty-based international law long held that the costs of negative externalities were to be borne by those who suffered from them, thus promoting irresponsibility. As will be discussed in chapter 6, it was up to the informal sanctions of reciprocity, retorsion, and reprisal to "enforce" responsibility.

Our hypothetical herdsmen's "right to pasture their cattle in the commons . . . is unmatched by a corresponding responsibility" (Hardin 1977b, 72). We similarly have tax evaders and people who feel it is not wrong to shoplift from large retail merchandisers or to rip off large insurance companies. The goods *appear* to be indivisible (and infinite), but there are costs, and everyone else has to pay them. The people who impose these costs on others, however, are not acting responsibly—they do not answer to those on whom they impose costs.

The types of goods that indeed are most often involved in commons situations are common-pool resources. In the global arena, they are natural resources that do not belong to any specific state, that do not fall under a state's sovereignty or jurisdiction. They include the deep seabed, the high seas, and their fisheries; outer space; the atmosphere, including the ozone layer; the carbon dioxide balance; and the electromagnetic frequency spectrum for broadcasting. Many people see the natural resources that exist on earth, even those within national boundaries (such as the Amazonian rain forests), as a "global commons." There are many such examples, including all of the nonrenewable energy resources like oil, natural gas, and coal. But who owns or has jurisdiction over such resources? Who should? By custom and law they are in fact usually privately owned, falling under the territorial jurisdiction (and thus sovereignty) of individual states. Some CPRs, such as the high seas and its resources, were for long periods of time seen as *res communis*—goods that belonged to everyone.[4]

Thus, one major way to look at common-pool resources (and at any good with externalities, such as collective goods) involves property rights and a "common property regime," where some form of authority outlines the rights, responsibilities, and relationships that the appropriators have with one another (see Bromley 1991; Hall 1996). The property rights of common-pool resources *cannot* be defined and enforced by economic means. To deal with the creation and distribution of rights and responsibilities in regard to property, ownership, usage—that is, jurisdiction—we must return again to social and political mechanisms.[5] In the international arena such mechanisms include international law and the more inclusive set of international regimes of which law is but one component. As will be elaborated subsequently and in Part 2 of this book, central to answering "how to manage interdependence?" is the relationship among diplomacy, law, and regimes. This relationship is key to how states adapt to, and shape, their environment.

All the world's resources are finite—they can be used up. The concern with global ecology and limits-to-growth issues are related to the tragedy of the commons. Factors such as population and technology are bases for the demands on the world's natural resources: water, air, arable land, and energy resources such as petroleum, coal, natural gas, and wood. They are also the bases for the pollution of air and water and the destruction of common-pool resources such as the ozone layer in the atmosphere, animal and fish species, forests, and topsoil. The world can and should be seen as a global commons. All the states on it, like the individuals Hardin describes, can through self-interest destroy a commons that already exists. This situation exposes another side of the metaphor of spaceship earth: a single, finite environment whose supplies can be consumed.

We must return to the "remorseless working of things." Economic growth and development is a dominating issue for all states. Development is a major issue between the rich and the poor. The powerful states must

---

4. And, going back to Hardin's discussion of responsibility, ownership by all implied the taking of responsibility by none.

5. Miller and Hammond (1994, 5) argue that, "Economic efficiency in the presence of externalities requires the resolution of a fundamentally political problem. . . ."

continue to grow, industrialize, and produce to stay powerful. Similarly, leaders in the developing countries often must put economic development and industrialization at the top of their list of objectives. Thus, most countries of the world desire resources, and this desire is becoming increasingly greater, not smaller. These resources, however, have to come from the global commons. A major concern of environmentalists is the consumption of finite resources at exponential growth rates, leaving the resource cupboard bare. Such processes have been in full swing in the destruction of whales and some fish stocks in the ocean. As recently as the mid-twentieth century blue whales, right whales, and bowhead whales numbered in the hundreds of thousands. Since the late 1980s these numbers have dropped to fewer than eight thousand. In the 1940s the global fish catch was 20 million tons; by the 1970s it had risen to 70 million tons. During this period, the world's fishing fleets quadrupled in size. But many species of fish have become scarce as a result of overfishing, many parts of the ocean have become so polluted that fish can no longer live there, and fish and seafood are threatened by local pollution disasters such as spills from oil tankers. The fishing problem is a striking example of the tragedy-of-the-commons process at work.

Collective Goods and the Prisoner's Dilemma

A second cut at the "remorseless working of things" involves the Prisoner's Dilemma. Again, we have the long-term interest of the group (and the individual as well) in opposition to the short-term interests of individuals. Why are problems like the free rider and the tragedy of the commons so prevalent in the international arena? One answer is simply the nature of that arena to the extent that it is based on the Westphalian system of states, each with sovereignty and no higher authority to tell it what to do—the anarchic system.

In this anarchic system, lack of trust is built into the relations among the international actors. Lack of trust gives each individual actor the dilemma of choosing between individual and collective welfare, creating the possibility of trusting others and then being taken advantage of by them. This situation is yet another version of the Prisoner's Dilemma, with the same predicament of temptation and trust. While the "anarchy" of the international system has been mentioned a number of times in this discussion, and will be central to subsequent chapters, note that it has *only now* appeared as important—not as the overriding element of system structure as in Waltz (1979), but only as an adjunct to the "meta-Prisoner's Dilemma" with which states must deal. The anarchic system, central to the Realist worldview, is indeed an important "permissive" condition that allows certain behavior to occur; nevertheless, it is a constant, while as scholars we wish to explain the variance in behavior.[6]

The Prisoner's Dilemma occurs when actors pursue short-term individual gain and benefit—what Keohane (1984, 99) terms "myopic self-interest"—over longer-term collective interest. This same process occurs with the free rider and the tragedy of the commons. Without a basis for trust, an actor in a Prisoner's Dilemma situation pursues individual benefits to avoid being caught as the sucker. In the original Prisoner's Dilemma scenario, the sucker is sent to jail for a long period of time, while the other prisoner serves a very short sentence. In an arms race, the sucker does not acquire more arms, while the opponent surges ahead; in an alliance, a major power spends large amounts on defense, while smaller allies pay little and take a free ride on alliance security. In a CPR situation the sucker stops hunting whales (to give them time to repopulate), but others (such as Japan in past years or Norway since 1993) continue hunting at such a pace that the whales will be hunted into extinction anyway, while the sucker fails to receive any of the profits in the process. Fife (1977) even notes the existence of a "killing the goose" syndrome. Here at least one appropriator harvests as much of an endangered resource as possible before it disappears. Acting "irresponsibly" (as defined earlier), such appropriators are not simply acting to prevent being a sucker, but to benefit their own long-term economic gain.

The formally anarchic nature of international relations in general may be characterized as a "meta-Prisoner's Dilemma" (see, for instance, Snyder 1971). The Prisoner's Dilemma is a pervasive social situation or structure of payoffs affecting choice (opportunity affecting willingness through incentive structures). Indeed, Jon Elster has defined politics as "the study of ways of transcending the Prisoners' Dilemma" (see Stein 1990, 33). This view is a partial answer to the question: is it possible to restructure the preferences of the parties involved in such a way that the Prisoner's Dilemma can be avoided and the collective goods produced? We also want to know: which approaches to international politics can give us the best purchase in addressing this problem?

These questions will be discussed at length in the following chapter. As a preview, note that many groups of various sizes and made up of different kinds of entities have discovered ways to solve the Prisoner's Dilemma. Following Taylor and Singleton (1993, 70), we should ask,

---

6. Even more problematic is the inability of anarchy-based Realist approaches to explain the nature of defection in a Prisoner's Dilemma—out of aggressive-offensive motives or defensive ones; or *when and why* defection *does not* occur! These questions will be addressed in chapter 4 and elaborated in Part 2.

"Why are some groups able to solve a collective action problem by themselves and others not?"

While not developed in depth in this volume, we must understand that to deal with the problems of interdependent externalities, the free rider and the tragedy of the commons, we must look across all levels of analysis and take into account the two-level games of domestic and international politics that policymakers must play simultaneously. We must deal with individual choice, collective choice, and "constitutional choice" (that is, the structure of rules and organizations). In so doing, however, the inadequacy of Realist, Structural Realist, and even Neorealist models becomes evident.

Japan, for instance, is not a single-minded, monolithic actor. A process of bureaucratic politics goes on within Japan that has made it very difficult for the Japanese government to change its whaling policies. We must remember, however, that certain policies, such as killing whales, may be very rational in terms of domestic political games and the domestic political stakes involved, but they appear much less rational from a global perspective. Although outsiders see these issues as negotiable economic objectives, some Japanese interests, such as the whaling companies, see them as issues of survival. Japanese government officials must try to satisfy or compensate those interests. Such differing perceptions make difficult problems more difficult still.[7]

One purpose of this chapter was to clarify the implications of interdependence for the study of international order. What are the consequences of collective goods? As an extreme form of interdependence and externality, collective goods create *special needs* for cooperation and collaboration, especially for sovereign states that must exist, coexist, and prosper within the anarchic Westphalian system. Collective goods can create conflict; they can prevent required actions from taking place; they can lead to the destruction of common-pool resources. These special needs, in turn, create *special problems* for establishing cooperation and collaboration: how to resolve the Prisoner's Dilemma by creating incentives for cooperation rather than noncooperation (through the temptation to defect). In their constant adaptation to the environment of the international system, states have engaged in the development of political mechanisms to deal with these problems: international law, international organizations, and international regimes. It is to these system "regulators" that we now turn.

---

7. This combination of domestic and external political issues is the central concern in George Tsebelis's 1990 analysis of nested games—that the outside observer may see another's behavior as irrational because the observer is watching only one game, while the policymaker is involved in several nested games and is behaving quite purposefully in dealing with them.

CHAPTER 4

Interdependence and Collective Goods: Mechanisms for Cooperative Management

Regulatory Mechanisms for Achieving Order in Anarchy

Having indicated in the last chapter the conditions that characterize interdependence, and the problems that the different forms of interdependence can generate for actors in the international system, we now turn to the ways by which states have attempted to adapt and deal with these conditions. And, how they have done so within the context of systemic anarchy.

States must act within an environment of formal anarchy—the absence of any formal authority situated above states—that promotes the meta-Prisoner's Dilemma. Still, there is order in anarchy. States and other international actors engage in many orderly interactions every day. Describing the international arena as anarchic, without a central authority, is not the same as saying that there are no organizations or rules to help organize and structure behavior. Reflecting the title of his book, *Cooperation under Anarchy,* Kenneth Oye (1986, 1) asks a central question: "If international relations can approximate both a Hobbesian state of nature and a Lockean civil society, why does cooperation emerge in some cases and not in others?"

As noted in Richard Rosecrance's 1963 classic (but underappreciated) study of the international system, *Action and Reaction in World Politics,* all international systems have *regulator mechanisms* to deal with disturbances in the system and the demands of its component units. Rosecrance argues that the stability of an international system depends on the balance between factors that disrupt the system and factors that regulate it. To keep any system stable, the regulators must be capable of dealing with the levels of disturbance in the system. In looking at the "mechanistic elements" of an international system, Rosecrance (1963, chap. 11) foreshadows many of the elements included in the opportunity-and-will-

43

ingness framework. Each system contains (1) sources of disturbance,[1] (2) regulators that arise and react to the disturbances, and (3) a set of environmental constraints, called a *table,* which converts the interaction of disturbance and regulator into (4) outcomes.

In chapters 1 and 3 I referred to the complex feedback loops that exist between the nature of the international system (primarily the consequences of interdependence, externalities, and collective goods) and the responses of states. The nature of the system affects the nature, behavior, and expectations of states—which in turn affect the nature of the system. The nature of states creates needs for order and regulation, leading to mechanisms such as law, organization, and norms—which in turn affect the environment or context within which states must behave.[2] The environment generates issues about which states interact; state interaction changes the environment and creates new issues. As with variations of opportunity and willingness, variations of this feedback loop can be found in other disciplines; for example, markets and the various economic interactions that take place within them. Rosecrance (1963, chap. 11) recognized this feedback loop when he argued that the "variety" of disturbances in the system "determines" the variety in the regulators. That is, the nature of needs, problems, and circumstances in the system creates a need for regulatory mechanisms to deal with them.

Looking across nine temporally defined international systems that he identified between 1789 and 1960, Rosecrance delineates such phenomena as the balance of power, the full and truncated Concert of Europe, alliance systems, the League of Nations, and the United Nations as system regulators.[3] He argues that regulative forces may be informal (such as the bal-

---

1. Much of the thinking about IR is concerned with the sources and nature of these disturbances. I have previously addressed such broad sources of disturbance as the differential growth (or decline) in power, the search for and extraction of resources, and lateral pressure models (both internal and external) in Starr 1994.

2. This feedback loop is the complex relationship between agent and structure that Wendt (1987) thought he solved with "structuration theory." However, as demonstrated in Friedman and Starr forthcoming, the nonrecursive relationship between agent and structure—that is, between opportunity and willingness—requires that one element *always* be exogenous. Such a feedback loop is continuous, and one's theoretical or research concerns will force the scholar to cut into the loop at *some* particular point. At *that point* either agent (willingness) or structure (opportunity) will be the exogenous independent variable (for want of a better term)—being the broader context that has an impact on the other.

3. K. J. Holsti (1992, 45–46) presents a list of activities that emanated from the nineteenth-century balance of power and concert, demonstrating *how* such regulators worked. For example, they produced "declarations announcing new norms or clarifying old ones," the "prevention of, or pre-empting unilateral actions," or the "introduction of conflict-resolving mechanisms and institutions." In chapter 6 we will look at the various functions of international law and see strong parallels to Holsti's discussion of the balance-concert.

ance of power) or formal (such as international organizations or regular systems of consultation as in the Concert). Following this basic view of regulators, we can see both formal and informal components, including state and nonstate actors. We are thus quite close to the more contemporary conceptual construct of *regimes.* More explicitly drawing upon transnational relations and regimes, Rosenau (1995) discusses a similar set of "steering mechanisms" of global governance. Thus, in response to interdependence and collective goods "disturbances," states have created regulatory mechanisms to maintain order in anarchy: organizations (states, IGOs, NGOs) and rules (informal norms, formal international law, the domestic laws of states, or municipal law) that can restructure the payoff matrix to help avoid the various forms of the Prisoner's Dilemma.

Strategies for Achieving Collective Goods

States in the current system have indeed overcome the pressures to defect in situations characterized by the Prisoner's Dilemma. Hence, there must be strategies to promote the international cooperation—coordination or collaboration—required to solve the problems posed by free riders and exploiters of the commons. As noted, collective goods present situations where the strictly economic forces of the marketplace cannot bring about solutions and where political and social action must be taken either to achieve desired collective outcomes or to prevent the destruction of common-pool resources. Six broad strategies for achieving collective goods will be presented here. All of them in some way work to change the incentive structures of the states involved—in some way acting either to *increase the costs of defecting* or to *increase the payoffs of cooperation.*[4]

1. An individual's preferences, or calculations of costs and benefits, can be changed—as any discussion of influence and leverage in social relations demonstrates—through punishment or reward. One way to get individuals to cooperate is through *coercion.* Yossarian, for example, was in the army because it was against the law to refuse to be drafted. While he was in the army, the army could threaten imprisonment, even execution, if he refused to fight. Within states, tax systems are backed up by threats of punishment for nonpayment (that is, for free riding). When a union achieves a union shop, it forces all workers to join the union, eliminating the free rider who would not join but would still enjoy most of the benefits, such as safe working conditions, obtained by the union from management.

This type of coercion is difficult in international relations because it

---

4. See Olson 1968 and Russett and Sullivan 1971 for general statements of strategies to deal with collective goods dilemmas.

stems from a hierarchical structure of authority, with formal (and legitimate) sanctions available to that authority. The power to tax is not readily given to IGOs because it is a threat to sovereignty (note, however, that the European Union has such authority in a number of areas). Sometimes it is possible for an individual state, such as the United States as a dominant alliance leader, to try to coerce its (cold war) allies to pay their share in an alliance (NATO). In this example, the United States would threaten to pull U.S. troops out of Europe. Coercion was an important element in the Soviet Union's management of burden sharing in the Warsaw Pact (see Starr 1974).

Thus, many analysts feel that coercion can occur only with a central authority given enforcement powers and that it is the only way to solve collective goods problems. Calls for some form of world government have been made on this basis. While such calls may be extreme, many issues can be handled by creating organizations that have been given authority by their constituent states, as in the creation of international regimes. For example, according to the 1982 Law of the Sea Treaty, the common-pool resources of the deep seabed, such as the metal-rich manganese or nickel nodules, were to be "owned" by the newly created International Seabed Authority. A more narrow but successful regime is overseen by the North Pacific Fur Seal Commission for the management of the harvesting of seals by the United States and Russia (with profits to be shared with Canada and Japan, which have agreed to refrain from hunting seals). The use of IGOs or regimes for self-constraint should indeed be seen broadly as coercion. In discussing how to manage a commons, Hardin (1977a, 26–27) reminds us, "The social arrangements that produce responsibility are arrangements that create coercion of some sort." For sovereign states, using the principles of utility and consent to guide their adherence to rules,[5] the important point is that such coercion is "mutual coercion mutually agreed upon."

As with sanctions in international law and regimes, the larger realm of coercive mechanisms in international politics is informal. The same holds with collective goods management strategies. Olson (1968) has argued that if a group is small, a free-riding member is more easily identified. If that can be done, then *social pressure* can be applied to encourage the member's cooperation. A government and its leaders may lose prestige if other governments feel that that they are not pulling their weight or cooperating or adhering to generally held norms. NATO's annual review to identify and spotlight slackers has been used in this way.

---

5. These principles are key elements to a "positivist" view of international law to be developed in this chapter and in chapter 6.

Similar pressure was put on states that bore low costs during the Gulf War or that dragged their feet in paying their share. In the area of the international law of human rights—with the development of universal norms—the "mobilization of shame" is a similar social pressure mechanism (e.g., see Soroos 1986, chap. 7).

As we review the range of coercive strategies, it should be noted that they cannot be characterized as purely Realist, Idealist, or strictly Liberal. In many ways such labels or categories are not relevant. These strategies and mechanisms take many combined and substitutable forms—all of which may be used to adapt to conditions of interdependence. While we can say the same of the broad strategies to follow, the point is most sharply made in discussing the use of coercion.

2. In general, positive strategies based on rewards of some kind seem to be more useful than negative ones in the international sphere.[6] Such strategies act to increase the benefits of cooperation, thus moving the payoff matrix away from the structure of the Prisoner's Dilemma. Members of a group will be more likely to act to obtain a collective good if they can receive *private goods as side payments.* States may join alliances and provide a share of the defense burden if they receive new and sophisticated weapons in return. States may refrain from exploiting a common-pool resource if offered other goods, profits, or a technology that can substitute for the resource. The most prominent example of such a strategy is the growing use of "debt-for-nature" swaps by which developed states and IGOs have traded debt payments from developing countries for reduction or cessation in the harvesting of tropical rain forests. The less developed countries (LDCs) receive the private good of forgiven debt (which increases the benefits of cooperation) for their protection of a global CPR—a CPR, however, that is found *within* the territory of sovereign states.

We noted Hardin's argument that the commons brings about irresponsible behavior in those who use it. In most CPRs, unlike the tropical rain forests, people have a right to the commons but rarely exercise responsibility in its use because it is large and impersonal and belongs to everyone. One way to foster responsibility is to convert parts of the commons into enclosed areas for which individual members are responsible—a process of privatization directed at removing the jointness of supply. Recipients must treat these enclosures with care, or else they will destroy their own property. It may thus be possible to save a common-pool resource by converting at least part of it into private goods by assigning

---

6. For example, see the series of works by Roger Fisher and colleagues on negotiation strategies and the types of incentives and offers that appear to work best; (e.g., Fisher 1969, Fisher and Ury 1981).

property rights. The most prominent example of such a privatization strategy in global politics is found in one outcome of the UN Law of the Sea Conference—the general acceptance of 200-mile-limit exclusive economic zones (EEZs). The EEZ extended the coastal jurisdiction of states to 200 miles for economic purposes. The aim was to evade the Prisoner's Dilemma by firmly assigning responsibility. In this way, a large part of the continental shelf and seabed and over 40 percent of the high seas were placed under regulation and restriction.[7]

Just as some analysts feel that the best way to solve collective goods problems is by coercion through the creation of central authority, others feel that privatization of some sort—creating private goods for the market to handle—is the best way to deal with collective goods, particularly the commons. In an argument that follows from public policy analyses developed and presented by the Ostroms two decades ago (Ostrom and Ostrom 1977), we too shall argue that there are middle-ground solutions. They are solutions that involve multiple and nested organizational arrangements and the development of behavioral norms accompanied by monitoring and sanctioning mechanisms. Once again, we find ourselves describing international regimes.

3. An additional consequence of privatization strategies is that sometimes the collective good is provided as a by-product of policies aimed at private goods. For example, if the states now controlling large EEZs take care of their own fisheries (for purely private reasons), they will, as a by-product, preserve the global fishery commons. Or, a state might create a large army for internal control or solely for its individual deterrence or defense. If it then joins an alliance, the alliance is provided with some forces that contribute to the collective good of a strong deterrent, even though that was not the first state's intention.

4. Another noncoercive strategy that could increase the incentives of cooperation is education to increase individual perceptions of the self-interest to be gained from group and long-term interests. This strategy clearly addresses the question raised in the previous chapter about how states could not act in their own interests. With policymakers (and analysts) immersed in a Realist perspective of world politics, it would not be hard to be concerned only with one's own "myopic self-interest." Such policymakers would need to be schooled in understanding that their best payoffs come in the long-term collective interests of cooperation. The preferability of mutual cooperation outcomes has been demonstrated in

---

7. Note also that a set of rules was created by the United Nations Conference on the Law of the Sea (UNCLOS III) for a variety of types of migratory fish species, under which the states agreed to limit the harvesting of such fish even within the EEZ (e.g., see Hall 1996).

the vast literature analyzing the Prisoner's Dilemma (e.g., see Axelrod 1984).

Using the Law of the Sea again to illustrate the point, Malta's representative to the General Assembly, Arvid Pardo, proposed in 1967 that the General Assembly deal with ways to extract the resources of the seabed in the interests of humanity as a whole, calling the seabed resources the "common heritage of mankind." Much of this educational task has taken place within the context of international organizations. It has been performed by experts, acting singly or collectively in both NGOs and IGOs. These groups of experts, or knowledge-based communities, are the epistemic communities studied by Peter Haas (1992). Educational tasks have also been undertaken by academics interested in world order or the environment, or by experts outside academia in such as groups as the Club of Rome.

Again, the intent behind this strategy is to force policymakers to confront the Prisoner's Dilemma and to understand what the structure of the decision situation looks like. If policymakers understand that their interests are best served in the long run, they will be better able to deal with these problems. They will also be better able to sell such cooperative strategies to the necessary domestic constituencies in this two-level game.

The educational strategy is also related to the process of integration that consists of shifting loyalties to new and larger political units with broader interests. But this is a slow process, and a number of our collective goods problems require immediate attention and quick action.

5. A collective good can be provided if one member of the group desires that good so much that it is willing to pay the whole cost (or most of it) by itself and does not care that other group members also receive the good. Olson (1968, 49–50) calls this a "privileged" group. In this case, one or more members of the group, in effect, offers to be the sucker. Besides valuing the good highly, such members are usually richer in resources than other members and thus can provide most of the collective good at much less sacrifice than could other members. Studies of UN budget assessments and burden sharing in alliances such as NATO and the Warsaw Pact show that the larger members will pay proportionately more to get the things they want, even if others free ride. Evidence for this behavior has included the U.S. desire to provide deterrence for itself and its NATO allies, possibly the U.S. role in stabilizing international trade, and even some tragedy-of-the-commons situations. For example, the maintenance of the upper atmosphere has collective goods properties. A very large state can be very effective in environmental control, both because it is big and rich and can therefore afford to bear the costs and because it can coerce some transnational actors to provide benefits to other countries.

An example of this kind of behavior is the U.S. government's 1978 ban on chlorofluorocarbon propellants in spray cans sold in the American market, a ban instituted to reduce depletion of the ozone layer in the world's atmosphere. That ban immediately set in motion a 50 percent reduction in world usage of such propellants (although the United States did not deal effectively with other uses of those chemicals, such as in plastic foam and in refrigerants). Moreover, some MNCs producing for many countries in the world market eliminated the propellants from their production, chiefly because it was cheaper not to use fluorocarbons at all than to make one product for sale in the United States and another for sale in countries with less rigorous restrictions. Another example is international airline safety regulations. The Federal Aviation Administration requires that all aircraft landing in the United States have elaborate safety equipment. Thus, foreign airlines contemplating U.S. flights must install the equipment no matter where their airplanes customarily land. Other countries thus get the free rider's safety benefits without having to make their own safety regulations. These are the kinds of circumstances in which it can be very helpful to have a dominant or hegemonic power in the system.

6. Returning to the "middle-ground" strategies noted in point 2, another mechanism for achieving collective goods is to create localized or regional organizations from a number of small groups of states and then to create some sort of federal structure to tie together and coordinate these groups. This approach involves the use of IGOs to address collective goods problems in ways that often follow the logic and processes of Ernst Haas's neofunctionalist model of integration. And, as we will discuss shortly, the use of IGOs (and NGOs) to create order and "governance" over specified functional or geographic areas is central to the concept of international regimes.

Keeping with the focus on regimes, note that these general strategies for coping with and resolving collective goods issues involve both formal and informal mechanisms. These mechanisms, involving both state and nonstate actors, help states coordinate their activities and collaborate in a *positive* way. Possible solutions to collective goods problems include appeals to self-limitation, mechanisms that facilitate communication and monitoring of behavior, a clear definition of the group, and mechanisms that facilitate the growth of norms for self-restraint and positive cooperation. While drawing from the international arena and large-scale international collective action problems, these conditions are similar to the ones identified by Elinor Ostrom (1990) in her analysis of the conditions under which a much smaller, local commons can be saved or destroyed (without centralized coercion or complete privatization).

The strategies just discussed—and which appear to work at both the international and local levels—only hint at a very powerful informal process that helps overcome the problem of the Prisoner's Dilemma/free rider/tragedy of the commons. The most problematic aspect of the Prisoner's Dilemma is trusting the other side in a specific situation. The situation of the players is clarified as they either defect or cooperate (or, in the actual Prisoner's Dilemma, immediately resolved by one or both going to jail). This is a *single-play situation.* But most relationships in social life, and certainly in international relations, are continuous. That is, there are multiple plays in any game, and it is possible for the players to learn what will happen to them if they defect in the dilemma. Axelrod's 1984 work has demonstrated that in experimental games, players did best following a tit-for-tat strategy: cooperating until the other player defected and then retaliating. The defecting player would then return to cooperation. If both players followed the never-defect-first principle, they could avoid the dilemma.

It thus may be possible to deal with the dilemma if there are many plays (an iterated Prisoner's Dilemma) and the players understand that there is an interdependent *reciprocity* in the play: you might be able to hurt the other player, but the other player can also hurt you. All plays of a game, even the Prisoner's Dilemma, are played under the "shadow of the future." That is, players can learn from past plays (history) and should be concerned with reciprocity in plays to come (future). Players thus come to understand that their own interests can only be met through the interdependent outcomes that result from the behavior of all players. The benefits of cooperation are highlighted through understanding the results of long-term cooperation that derive from attending to long-term collective interests. "Trust" may develop (as in Deutschian integrational models). But, trust is less important than each player understanding that mutual interests are served by cooperation (the positivist view of international law). The reciprocity of tit for tat also makes it clear that there will be costs imposed—sanctions—when there is defection. Therefore, we find both increased payoffs from cooperation and increased costs for defection.

Reciprocity is even more important when we recall that there are many games being played at the same time, that states interact in many issue areas at the same time, and that these areas are *linked,* especially as interdependence becomes tighter. A state may defect in one game (for example, arms control) but will have to worry about the other player's defection in another (retaliatory acts in trade, wheat sales, alliance formation, military spending). It must be remembered that all states need things from other states. In this regard almost all actors have some form of leverage (rewards or punishments) that can be utilized against other states.[8] The payoff matrix of costs and benefits thus will be affected by calculations of future costs and benefits. This menu will then affect the willingness of policymakers to defect.

These ideas of reciprocity (especially as sanctions that can impose costs for defecting) are central to understanding the workings of international law and the importance of regimes—formal and informal rules and expectations—in the interdependence among international actors. As Elizabeth Zoller notes, reciprocity "is a condition theoretically attached to every legal norm of international law" (quoted in Keohane 1989, 132). Reciprocity also helps explain how we can have order and certain amounts of stability and predictability in formally anarchic situations (this idea will be expanded in chapter 6).

International Cooperation and International Law: A Brief Introduction

To begin solving collective goods problems (or other problems affecting more than one state), states need to cooperate and interact in a smooth, regularized manner. Increasingly, the transnational issues of the contemporary world—economic and ecological—require action by more than one state. States need one another's aid to solve common problems in an era of interdependence. The paradox, of course, is that although states often cooperate on the basis of self-interest, the heart of the collective goods issue is the need to see the connection between individual state interests and the longer-term collective interests of the group.

States need one another. They need to carry on regularized relations with one another, through diplomacy, for example. Traditional bilateral diplomacy must be augmented by other mechanisms to maintain and increase regular, smooth interactions of states. International law is such a mechanism. While international law cannot solve all our global problems, neither is it irrelevant to the activities of states. International law must be seen within a political context, within the historical context of the Westphalian state system that created international law in its modern form, and within contemporary international politics. But this view is the reciprocal interaction noted earlier. Politics creates law, and law shapes the form of future politics by serving as part of the menu within which future politics must occur.

Very simply, most states usually do conform to the rules of international law. In that respect, international law acts in the same way as

---

8. See North and Choucri 1983 for a discussion of leverage; see Baldwin 1985 for discussions of exchange and influence.

domestic law, as a set of rules that constrain behavior. This view and the study of international law since the nineteenth century reflect a positivist view of international law, which holds that international law is created by people and that the obligation to follow law is based on self-interest, utility, and especially consent. Law is what states agree to and is based on the behavior of states. This view helps us understand why international law works: it has been created to help states interact smoothly. This positivist view gives international law a certain degree of legitimacy. International law can regulate behavior because it is based on the self-constraint of states. If we understand that international law has many functions, including a coordinating and facilitating function similar to civil law on the domestic level, then we can see it as "law." Compared with domestic law, international law is "relatively decentralized." Another scholar says simply, "International law should be regarded as true but imperfect law" (von Glahn 1981, 4).

States pay great attention to international law (for example, the legal adviser's staff at the U.S. State Department reviews most of the department's work). However, if the fear of enforcement by armed agents of a central authority is not the cause of states' conforming to rules, what is? Again, remember that nothing is distributed evenly in the international system. The great bulk of world politics and transnational interaction consists of the exchange of goods, services, people, and information. All states benefit from this regular and routine flow of people, goods, and information. Thus, states see it as in their own self-interest to constrain their behavior according to the rules of international law, most of which eases and routinizes such interaction. Foreign policy behavior that violates international norms is less probable because of the costs entailed. States follow international law both from the fear of chaos and from the fear of retaliatory punishment (reciprocity). The other side of the coin, of course, is a state's desire to appear to be a law-abiding citizen in the international community, to be a state that others can depend upon and trust. This sort of reputation will enhance a state's influence through the *golden rule condition:* if a state behaves correctly, it can expect to receive good behavior from others.

As will be amplified in chapter 6, contrary to an extreme Realist's belief, states do acknowledge international law and are constrained by it. Leaders justify their behavior in terms of international law and in questionable cases try to indicate that their behavior conforms to international law (in the immediate case and other areas). The Reagan administration, which was accused of disregarding international law in Grenada, in the mining of Nicaraguan waters, and in the April 1986 bombing of Libya, nevertheless made a great effort to contend that such behavior was permitted within the rules of international law. The Bush administration acted similarly during the December 1989 military intervention in Panama. It justified its action by arguing that it protected U.S. citizens, protected the canal, restored democracy to Panama, and was needed to arrest dictator Manuel Noriega on drug charges. This action was code named "Operation Just Cause" in an attempt to appeal to the theory of just war. States understand that breaking international law imposes costs on them.

International law, then, serves a number of functions in helping states create and preserve order, including conflict resolution and control but also more important communication, socialization, and coordination or management functions. These international legal functions apply to all matters involving international politics. International law specifies which actors are "legal persons" having the capacity to enter legal relations.[9] International law deals with questions of territory and nationality: which territory and people belong to which state, what states are allowed to do on their own territory and on the territory of others, and what states can do with their own people and to aliens (nationals of other countries). International law covers the broad range of peaceful interactions between states, including treaties (law on how to make law), diplomacy (law on how to conduct foreign relations), and the creation and work of IGOs. All areas of commerce and economic interaction are also affected by treaties and by IGOs and their activities. International law has always been concerned with the broad issues of war, from questions of aggression and the legality of war to questions of intervention, terrorism, the conduct of war, the legality of certain weapons, and arms control.

International law thus becomes a component in the incentive structures of states. In so doing it becomes part of the environment or context within which states must act. Norms and principles—either informal or formally specified in treaties—change, develop, disappear. They are thus elements of the environment that alter the opportunities available to any actor at any given point in time. These opportunities—constraints but also enabling principles—affect the costs and benefits of behavior and thus the willingness of leaders to take certain actions.

International Cooperation and International Organizations: A Brief Introduction

States engaging in diplomacy create treaties, which add considerably to the body of international law. Many of these treaties also create international

---

9. This definition of "legal persons" is one of the areas in which the statecentric bias of international law is most clearly demonstrated.

organizations, so that IGOs are a product of international law. However, in yet another reciprocal relationship, the growing number of IGOs also feeds back to be one of the primary sources of international law in the contemporary system. The charters of these organizations—their rules, agreements, resolutions, and treaties—constitute many of the bylaws of everyday international interaction. Some IGOS, such as the UN (through the work of the International Law Commission), have helped to codify, collect, and apply international law derived not only from IGOs but from treaties, custom, and the work of international courts. IGOs have been useful in applying international law, in helping to coordinate states' compliance, in organizing states around their common interests, and in pointing out the benefits of cooperation. Large regional organizations such as the European Union have worked extensively to promote economic cooperation. Others, such as the Organization of American States and the Organization of African Unity, have worked to control and manage conflict in their regions.

Realists usually see IGOs as of little importance; proponents of transnational or globalist perspectives see them as more useful, if not now, then in the future. In thinking about IGOs in relation to international order, we need to stress their formal nature: they are created by two or more states (and possibly other IGOs or NGOs) by a formal constitution or instrument that establishes some form of continuous administrative structure. This formal structure then seeks to pursue the common interests of the members in ways that reflect the aforementioned strategies to deal with collective goods issues.

First, and very important, an IGO provides a forum where states can interact with each other diplomatically at a permanent site. It also aids cooperation by providing a permanent mechanism for addressing policy issues. States expect the IGO to help with certain problems; for example, the World Health Organization with disease control, or UNESCO with education.

Also, an IGO often collects and makes available a great deal of information on specific problems and on its member states. UN publications, for instance, provide voluminous data on a wide variety of economic, demographic, social, cultural, and political matters. This information may be crucial in complex coordination or problem-solving situations. When regimes are created to help deal with collective action problems, and especially CPRs, some organization must be responsible for providing information on the amount of the resource available, what the harvesting capacity and rate should be, projections of resource usage and availability, and so on.

Finally, IGOs also perform regulative and distributive functions.

IGOs distribute things, such as billions of dollars in loans from the World Bank or court decisions from the International Court of Justice. IGOs also make and administer rules on how states should behave in certain areas—from the IMF in monetary policy to the UN in regard to the use of force or the treatment of political prisoners to the European Union on almost every area of economic interaction of its members. The EU may be termed *supranational,* an IGO with the power to act separately from the member states and to make decisions that are binding on their members even if some members disagree. Such IGOs indeed appear to take aspects of members' sovereignty away from them. In the evolution of the European Union, various organs of that organization have developed extensive independent powers. The EU is apparently the only true supranational IGO in the current global system (see Archer 1994).

It is important to note that states *use* both international law and IGOs as *instruments* to further their own foreign policy interests. States use international law and IGOs to legitimize or justify their behavior, to pursue diplomacy, and to increase their individual influence as well. We need to be clear that in the Westphalian system, international law and IGOs (and perhaps most important, the United Nations) are only as successful as the member states want them to be. They are only as successful as they are perceived to be. That is the essence of Stanley Hoffmann's "mirror" metaphor, which sees international law or organization as merely a magnifying mirror that "faithfully and cruelly" reflects the realities of world politics (1972, 431).

The mirror metaphor is a necessary consequence of the international law–international politics feedback loop. International law is one of the main mechanisms by which the state attained its central place as an international actor; international law legalized the very existence of states. In essence, it created the rules and conditions that permit the individual state, as well as the international system, to survive.

The United Nations System

Besides being a major source of international law and the most extensive system of international organization in the contemporary world (in both the extent of its membership and the broad scope of its aims and activities), the United Nations is also one of the most faithful of the mirrors that reflect the nature of international politics. The founders of the United Nations were (R)ealists enough to recognize that the organization was to be composed of sovereign states, and they did not see the United Nations as a device to take away or undercut their sovereignty—although some later observers have argued that that should be the UN's role. On the other hand, since the international system was composed of sovereign states and lacked a central authority, one strategy for promoting international cooperation was the creation of a universal IGO. Their realism was tempered by enough idealist vision to seek new international institutions and procedures to promote common interests and manage conflict. Mechanisms to coordinate behavior and promote cooperation became even more crucial as international interdependences multiplied and as collective goods issues became prominent. Perhaps one reason for the remarkable survival of the United Nations beyond its fiftieth anniversary has been its utility in an era when environmental, economic, and ethical issues have become central in a system with many new international actors and a more sensitive and vulnerable set of international interdependences.

The changing nature of the United Nations has been influenced by the nature of its new members. Many of these newer UN members are independent in part because of the work of the Trusteeship Council, which was established to bring an end to colonialism and to guide the former colonial areas to independence as peacefully as possible. Most observers agree that the Trusteeship Council fulfilled its purpose well. The Economic and Social Council is assigned the task of dealing with international economic, social, educational, and health matters. It is supposed to improve the world's living standards by attacking poverty, ignorance, and inequality as causes of war. Many health matters have been successfully dealt with; many educational and cultural dissemination programs have also had positive results.

A newly developed superpower cooperation has been a central motor to change in the international environment:

> There have always been connections between the general climate of world politics and the functioning of the United Nations, but the usual impacts have been negative. During the cold war years, and during times of North-South confrontation, political conflict in the world was registered as political stalemate in the United Nations. Now, political settlement in the world is being registered as political cooperation among the major powers in the United Nations. The results of this cooperation are manifest in a re-invigoration of the United Nations Security Council, a new and mutually supportive relationship between the Secretary-General and the permanent members of the Security Council, and, most dramatically, the initiation of several new UN peacekeeping operations . . . It is unlikely that any of these UN steps could have been taken unless the world

political climate changed in the way it did. . . . (Puchala and Coate 1989, 100)[10]

The United Nations Charter identified international peace and security as the UN's first goal, with economic and social cooperation and human rights as other objectives. In 1945 the founders of the United Nations envisaged a large role for the organization in collective security. Chapter VII, Articles 39–46 of the UN charter call on all members to make available to the Security Council, by special agreements, armed forces and facilities "for the purposes of maintaining international peace and security." These forces were to provide the basis for UN-authorized military actions against aggressor states. Almost immediately, however, the Cold War began and Soviet-U.S. hostility made it impossible for the permanent members of the Security Council to concur on the terms for a UN military force. In its first forty-five years, the UN only once designated a state as an aggressor; that was North Korea, in 1950, and the designation was made while the Soviet representative was boycotting the Security Council.

Not until 1990, after the Iraqi occupation of Kuwait, was collective security again invoked. Then the United States and the Soviet Union were in substantial agreement, and careful negotiations between them, China, Japan, and the other major European powers made possible the UN-authorized military actions against Iraq. There was, of course, no standing UN military force for those operations. Rather, a multinational coalition was assembled on an ad hoc basis. In practice the United States dominated the coalition and substantially controlled military and political strategy; the UN exercised only very general supervision. As in Korea, the response was ad hoc, and no formal or permanent procedures were developed. It remains to be seen whether the Gulf War will serve as a precedent for similar peace-enforcement operations in the future, or even serve to stimulate creation of some sort of UN permanent military capability that might also act as a deterrent to aggression; (see especially Russett and Sutterlin 1991). A "new world order" built around the concept of collective security might well be grounded in a renewed and expanded role for the UN.

The other kind of operation in which the UN can employ military force in order to manage threats to the peace and provide elements of order to areas of conflict is *peacekeeping.* Peacekeeping is very different from military peace enforcement: its purpose is conflict management or

---

10. For discussions of reforming the UN in order to reflect the needs and challenges of the post–cold war world as it approaches the twenty-first century, see Rochester 1993, Coate 1994, and Kennedy and Russett 1995.

settlement, and it does not involve assigning guilt or identifying an aggressor. Rather, it involves recognition that a violent conflict or threat to peace is at hand. Here the role of the UN is to stop fighting already under way, separate the warring parties, and create conditions for them to negotiate instead of fight. During the cold war the UN had little success with conflicts involving both superpowers because each could veto any proposed UN action. It was often more successful, however, in dealing with medium and minor powers in situations where the superpowers were not strongly involved on opposite sides.

Beginning with the Suez crisis in 1956, the UN dispatched lightly armed peacekeeping forces of varying magnitude to many trouble spots. These operations rarely included troops from the superpowers and were carried out only with the consent of the conflicting parties. The key to many of these operations was the use of UN forces to separate the armies of the warring parties and to maintain a cease-fire. The importance of such activities was made painfully clear in 1967, when Secretary-General U Thant acceded to the request by Egypt's President Nasser to remove the UN forces that had been stationed on the Sinai border between Israel and Egypt (but on Egyptian territory) since the Suez War. Israel's decision to launch the "preemptive" strike of the 1967 Six-Day War was strongly influenced by the absence of a UN barrier to a possible Egyptian attack, which the Israelis believed to be imminent.

The UN's original peacekeeping role—standing between hostile forces—has been expanded to include maintaining security or stability within a wide area (as in southern Lebanon), providing humanitarian assistance (Cyprus), disarming insurgents (Nicaragua), and monitoring elections (Namibia, Nicaragua, and Haiti). Gradually, therefore, the UN has become important in managing conflicts *within* a single country rather than purely between countries and has taken on a role in helping to secure peaceful transitions of government. It (and some regional international organizations, notably the Organization of American States) is increasingly helpful in easing the establishment of democratic governments, again, when the parties involved want such help.

For all its failures and limitations, the United Nations has become a powerful instrument for achieving human security in its broadest sense. While it has not satisfied all high hopes at the end of the cold war, it has accomplished far more than its detractors recognize, and more than many of its member governments. The UN consists of organs devoted to three different broad purposes, but organs that, as in a human body, complement each other and cannot be effective alone. These three organs are what Bruce Russett has called the "Three United Nations."

The most obvious UN is the UN of security against violence. It is the

UN of the Security Council, with its powers of peacekeeping, to apply economic sanctions and to carry out collective security operations against aggressors like Iraq. The second UN—of economic security and the provision of basic human needs—is less obvious. It is the UN of the specialized agencies and much of the Secretariat. It is the UN of emergency humanitarian assistance, of the Food and Agriculture Organization (FAO), the World Health Organization (WHO), and the United Nations Development Program; it is also the UN of the IMF and the World Bank, affiliated organizations disposing of enormous capital resources. Least visible, but equally important, is the UN of security of human rights. It is the UN that oversaw the treatment and ultimately the transition of trusteeships such as Namibia. It is the UN of the International Court of Justice, of the Electoral Assistance Unit of the Secretariat, of the High Commissioner of Human Rights, the High Commissioner for Refugees, and of the Universal Declaration of Human Rights.

The United Nations in its varied guises has attempted to deal with serious environmental, economic, and political problems, which may ultimately be the most crucial the world faces because of the interdependences of the world system. The three UNs have a synergy; they reinforce and build on each other. There can be little economic security if there is no security against violence, within countries as well as between them. Peacebuilding, in the wake of conflict, requires reestablishing economic security and protection of human rights for the vanquished, for minorities, and for majorities that govern democratically.

Regimes and International Order

If states and other international actors are to cooperate and deal with the Prisoner's Dilemma posed by collective goods, how should they organize themselves? There are, as we have seen, a number of strategies for achieving collective goods. One method, in the words of Kindleberger (1981, 252), is to "bind the members of the international community to rules of conduct, to which they agree, and which will restrain each member from free riding, and allocate burdens equitably, as a matter of international legal commitment."

International law can do that, but the rules of conduct that affect international behavior go beyond those of international law. International law does not exist by itself; neither does international organization. Some groups of states and groups of activities exhibit strong elements of international order. Scholars have used the term *regime* to identify the *complete set of rules* that relate to the "governance" of some specified area of international relations. This concept helps us understand the full array of constraints imposed by international society. Standard definitions of regimes sees them as networks of "rules, norms and procedures that regularize behavior and control its effects . . . sets of governing arrangements" (Keohane and Nye 1989, 19) and "principles, norms, rules, and decision making procedures around which actor expectations converge in a given issue area" (Krasner 1983, 2). The regularization of behavior means the creation of patterns—patterns of procedures, patterns of compliance to norms and rules, and most especially, patterns of *expectations:* "What these arrangements have in common is that they are designed not to implement centralized enforcement of agreements, but to establish stable mutual expectations about others' patterns of behavior" (Keohane 1984, 89).

What do these arrangements consist of, and where do these common understandings come from? There are formal components and informal components; there are national components, transnational components, and international components. The set of governing arrangements consists of national rules (the domestic laws of states), international rules (international law, the charters of IGOs, and the regulations, resolutions, and practices of IGOs), and private rules (the practices of MNCs and other NGOs, the charters of MNCs, and other formal regulations). They are the formal products of governments, IGOs, and NGOs. Regimes also include the norms and principles that reflect patterns of behavior not yet formally codified in law or organization. The development of international law through custom—the actual practice of states that is accepted as law—is an important example of informal norms that act as rules to constrain behavior. Norms, principles, and customary law all have a major psychological component in that the policymakers of states *feel* they should act in certain ways because they are expected to (and expect others to), whether or not a rule has been formalized by treaty.

Thus, we have sets of governing arrangements relating to various issue areas in international relations. Issue areas may be functional and thus be very wide or very narrow, paralleling the structure of functional IGOs. Young (1980, 331) notes simply, "We live in a world of international regimes." Their concerns range from monetary issues to trade issues, to the management of natural resources, to the control of armaments, to the management of power, to the management of outer space and the seabed. Regimes may also be geographic, covering problems that arise within a specific area; Antarctica presents such an example. Just as with IGOs, some regimes have only a few members, like that overseeing North Pacific fisheries, while some are very large, such as the UN conflict-management regime (see also Kratochwil and Ruggie 1986).

Much of the regime literature looks at economic or ecological issues. We need to recognize, however, that regimes apply to any set of rules, norms, expectations, and organizations that deal with a common issue or problem. When created to help manage common-pool resources, international management regimes act to create order in areas of market failure—where a market mechanism cannot work by itself and the tragedy of the commons is a potential threat. Many such regimes (e.g., those dealing with the seas and its fisheries) are, as noted, about property rights. They involve such issues as who is in the group, and thus is allowed to use some resource; how much of some resource is available ("harvesting capacity") and the rate at which it can be used; and how the benefits of some resource are to be distributed among the participants. Wijkman's 1982 example of all three in action involves the North Pacific Fur Seal regime, based around a 1957 convention negotiated by the United States, the Soviet Union, Japan, and Canada.[11] To prevent extinction of the seals, the agreement banned open-sea hunting, limited hunting to certain islands, and set quotas for yearly harvests—with a North Pacific Fur Seal Commission determining what the maximum yearly harvest would be. More interesting, Japan and Canada agreed to abstain from hunting seals, in return for being given a share of the profits by the United States and the Soviet Union (later Russia).

In her study of design principles for the maintenance of local but long-enduring CPR management institutions, Elinor Ostrom (1990, 90) outlines a variety of functions that regimes could fulfill, including "clearly defined boundaries," meaning the definition of *who* is permitted to consume the CPR. This idea is similar to the allocation of user rights. International law and IGOs help foster precision and provide the formal documents (treaties) that specify who is allowed to do what, including belong to the "group." A central component of Ostrom's design is the "monitoring" of CPR activity—auditing the activity of CPR users and the condition of the resource as well. Such monitoring is one of the primary functions of most IGOs, and especially those created for CPR management, such as the North Pacific Fur Seal Commission. Regimes are also well suited as "conflict-resolution mechanisms," as "low cost arenas to resolve conflicts among appropriators . . ."

Perhaps most important for our discussion here is Ostrom's point regarding CPRs that exist as parts of larger systems, as are the CPRs normally studied by IR scholars. She notes that for such CPRs there should be

---

11. As noted in Wijkman 1982, a "paradigm" for international management regimes includes (1) allocation of user rights, (2) distribution of pecuniary benefits, and (3) determination of harvesting capacity. Wijkman notes that the fur seal regime exemplifies a management regime for a CPR: "an efficient allocation and enforcement of harvesting rights, an acceptable distribution of the resource rents among the interested parties, and a scientifically determined harvesting quota" (526).

"nested enterprises": "Appropriation, provision, monitoring, enforcement, conflict resolution, and governance activities are organized in multiple layers of nested enterprises" (1990, 90).[12] Regimes—with their multiple actors working at multiple levels (the whole variety of transnational actors)—at least approximate such nested enterprises. Exactly how much may be borrowed from the study of local CPR management and in what ways global or regional CPR commons are similar or different from local CPRs are questions still under close scrutiny (see especially Keohane, McGinnis, and Ostrom 1993 and Keohane and Ostrom 1995).

Hegemony and Regimes

At the end of World War II, the Western powers were agreed in their basic views of the international economy. The cornerstone of their vision was a liberal system, one without the economic barriers that had been set up in the 1930s. It was to be a relatively unhampered economic system based on capitalism, the free market, and minimal barriers to trade. To make the system work, states had to cooperate. Establishing this system was seen as a major step toward creating peace and order in the world, particularly within the group of Organization for Economic Cooperation and Development (OECD) states. Free trade, free movement of capital, and stable monetary relations all depended on an orderly world. Thus, there was an interdependence between military and economic factors. The area had to be militarily secure from outside threats as well as internally peaceful. The same state that could provide military order—the United States—was also the only state economically strong enough to provide order to the economic system. As the source of economic growth, the United States was the "engine" of global economic development.

"Leadership" in the creation, maintenance, and effectiveness of regimes has been, and continues to be, an issue of debate. In the post–World War II international system based on U.S. military and economic predominance, the United States followed a policy of leadership, or, as some observers describe it, hegemony. In a hegemonic system, "one state is able and willing to determine and maintain the essential rules by which relations among states are governed. The hegemonial state not only can abrogate existing rules or prevent the adoption of rules it opposes but can also play the dominant role in constructing new rules" (Bergsten, Keohane, and Nye 1975, 14).

---

12. Scharpf's observation is a useful summary of our look at this middle-ground approach: "The existence of cooperative network structures will facilitate forms of positive and negative self-coordination that *are quite similar* to those produced within hierarchical organizations" (1994, 49; emphasis added).

Some analysts claim the problem today is that interdependence has grown and is outpacing the ability of states to manage it, and that that is due in large part to the decline of the United States as the protector. This view stems from arguments that hegemony can be a useful, if not a necessary, mechanism for helping a group achieve collective goods. Such was the case in Olson's privileged group where a larger or wealthier member provides the collective good for the whole group. Similarly, Kindleberger (1981, 252) argues that a stable world economy needs a "stabilizer." Frohlich, Oppenheimer, and Young (1971) suggest that a group needs an "entrepreneur" to provide the political leadership necessary to help the group achieve the collective goods it desires. In sum, these views argue that whether or not a collective good is supplied, the effectiveness and the stability of the group are affected by the presence or absence of a hegemon. This argument complements the view that much regime change is related to the appearance or disappearance of a hegemon.[13]

A related perspective on hegemony was provided by Karl Deutsch. Deutsch et al. (1957) suggested that one helpful condition in continuing the process of integration that would lead to a peaceful security community is a strong "core area" with "the capacity to act—a function of size, power, economic strength, and administrative efficiencies." Note that this core would provide resources to deal with demands in a manner quite similar to the way in which Rosecrance saw regulators dealing with disturbances.

It is doubtful that the existence of a large core area is essential to the kind of security community that exists among OECD countries, which have an even more stable condition of peace among themselves now, when the United States is much less predominant than just after World War II. Nevertheless, earlier U.S. predominance may have been very important in setting in motion the economic prosperity and interdependence that now underlie that peace. In this sense there is some virtue in having one big power in the international system: if it chooses, it can not only bully others but also make short-term sacrifices that will in the long run benefit all members, not just itself. The real problem in the identification and existence of a hegemon, however, has been pointed out by Kindleberger: distinguishing between leadership and domination. The utility and desirability of having a hegemon may very well depend upon where states sit in the

---

13. There are a number of skeptical viewpoints regarding the hegemon argument: whether or not a hegemon is *necessary* for regime creation, or especially whether or not a hegemon is necessary for regime maintenance, or whether or not there have actually been states that correspond to the characteristics of a "hegemon." See, for instance, Russett 1985 or Strange 1983. See Chan 1993 also for an overview of hegemony arguments.

international economic system. Developing countries that are dependent upon that hegemony and that see it as domination will have views very different from those of developed industrialized states, which see it as leadership.

Conclusions: The Utility of Regimes

If issue areas are characterized by interdependence, sets of governing arrangements will thus help those actors collaborate and coordinate their actions. Whatever the weaknesses, shortcomings, or costs of the regime components and arrangements, we must keep in mind Hardin's observation that "an alternative to the commons need not be perfectly just to be preferable" (1977a). For example, until the very end of the process, when the newly installed Reagan administration intervened, this attitude appeared to be a central component of the consensus over procedures and substance created by the participants in UNCLOS III.

Regimes, like international law, can help actors collaborate and coordinate to deal with collective action problems by changing the structure of payoffs, making cooperation more beneficial and defection more costly. Regimes can make sidepayments easier (as in sharing the fur seal profits with nonharvesters) and reduce transaction costs: "International regimes do not substitute for reciprocity; rather they reinforce and institutionalize it . . . delegitimizing defection and thereby making it more costly" (Axelrod and Keohane 1986, 250).

We have noted that integration is a positive mechanism for dealing with interdependence. Integration has been conceived as both a process and a result of cooperation. In particular, scholars identified with the approach of Ernst Haas, who take a functional view of integration, look to the formation of new and bigger states (amalgamation) as the result of integration. That has not happened. However, the logic of the functionalist approach *still* leads us to expect the development of functional cooperative structures among states. Regimes like those that have developed among the OECD countries, or even among the states of the European Union, are still relatively informal structures.

Rather than the formal creation of new states, we have other end products of integration. The Deutschian theory of integration, as will be developed later, is particularly open as to the nature of the products of integration.[14] The creation of new international organizations, new pat-

---

14. Puchala (1981, 156) notes that as a theory of integration, "Deutsch's formulation is valuable in as much as it focuses attention on international community formation during unification . . . Deutsch's formulations allow for a number of possible end-products. . . ."

terns of interaction among state and nonstate actors, and formal and informal rules and norms that govern behavior may all be seen as the results of integrative processes. That is, while the process of integration must be attended to continually, we can look at regimes as one set of phenomena that can be produced by integration processes. Regimes—areas of order, governance, and peace—are one type of end product of integration.[15]

In the debate over the similarity of local CPR management arrangements to those at the international level, some scholars argue that the "heterogeneity" of international actors, as well as the problems of scale make the two arenas quite different; that, in Snidal's (1995, 51) words, "the IR sociopolitical environment *appears* very different from various CPR settings" (see contributors to Keohane and Ostrom 1995). However, Snidal (1995, 65–66) also offers "community" as a plausible factor in the reduction of heterogeneity needed to help solve collective action problems. It should be clear that much of the discussion of local CPR management is about the nature and level of *integration* within the group involved, and how it relates to the mechanisms created to deal with local CPRs: the creation of mutual rewards, the learning of ways to manage their mutually shared problems, and the creation of new loyalties or identities.

If regimes are seen as one possible end product of integration processes—and both Deutschian and Haasian models see that end product exhibiting new patterns of loyalty, legitimacy, and *community*—then regimes could also be seen as a mechanism to promote the community used to solve global CPR problems. And thus, rather than stress scale or heterogeneity, scholars interested in how much can be borrowed across arenas—and thus how alike the CPR situations really are—should be focusing on conditions of integration such as community and responsiveness, and how well different types of regime structures both foster and reflect these conditions.

In general, the complex set of arrangements found in regimes may be the most promising way to achieve coordination and collaboration in an interdependent world system. Those arrangements are easiest to establish when one dominant state (a hegemon) can set forth the basic principles and enforce them. When hegemony wanes, there is a danger that the arrangements become fragile and harder to hold in place among compet-

---

15. Note that in his discussion of social systems, Deutsch (1977) indicated that we could analytically demarcate systems or subsystems from each other by looking for system boundaries. Such lines of demarcation would indicate "marked discontinuities" in patterns of behavior across the boundary. It is clear from this description that regimes can be bounded by such "marked discontinuities," indicating a different set of behaviors and interactions among regime members than between regime members and other actors.

ing interests. With waning hegemony it becomes even harder to replace the old arrangements (regimes) with new and more suitable ones—but that is precisely the challenge facing the world in the twenty-first century with new conditions and new demands on the Westphalian trade-off. In Part 2 we will investigate, from several different perspectives, the Westphalian trade-off and its impact on how states manage interdependence.

Part 2

CHAPTER 5

The State in a Multicentric/
Transnational World

One theme raised in the introduction was the examination of what is new and what is constant. This theme is essential to understanding environmental contexts and how international actors adapt to and manage those contexts. Theorists of international politics are fond of questioning the relevancy and continued existence of the "state," but most do so without explicitly considering the environment in which states must act in conjunction with the ways in which that environment may or may not actually be changing.

This chapter will begin with one of the most popular arguments about the decline of the state—its irrelevancy in a world dominated by transnational economics. By considering how entities adapt to environments, as well as what is actually new, or constant (especially in the relationship between politics and economics), I hope to provide a more balanced view of the continued place of the state in world politics. Without attempting to argue the Realist position, flaws in various transnational/pluralist/Liberal arguments will be highlighted. And finally, with this focus on new-or-constant, I will now introduce explicitly the concept of "sovereignty" into our discussion.

Demise of the Territorial State Revisited, Again[1]

Given the "turbulence" of the contemporary world arena, the rise of globalist or pluralist or transnational approaches to the global system, discussions over the rise of economic factors and the dominance of the global agenda by economic issues—and thus a debate over the very nature of "power"—we find analysts trying to disentangle the relationship between economics and politics. In looking at the transnational nature of multinational corporate enterprises and markets, analysts such as Stephen Kobrin

---

1. Note that this section head combines and paraphrases the two articles by John Herz written a decade apart: "The Rise and Demise of the Territorial State" (1957) and "The Territorial State Revisited—Reflections on the Nature of the Nation-State" (1968).

(1991, 1997) raise doubts as to the continuing importance of political borders in an economically transnational world. Given the transnational integration of markets, such scholars inquire as to the relevance and viability of territorially based sovereign units.

In chapter 2 we reviewed the importance of interdependence and transnationalism in the study of world politics. One of the main instruments by which economic interdependences have increased is the multinational corporation (MNC). In noting that MNCs (also called transnational corporations, or TNCs) have been seen as a challenge to the nation-state, I highlighted the tension that exists between transnational production and loyalty to any particular state. The standard view is that, to be regarded as a state, an entity requires at a minimum: territory, population, and a government that represents the state. Some form of nationalism is requisite to bond the people to one another and to the government. Such loyalty is the basis of nationalism; yet many observers support the position of Kobrin by noting that MNCs are careful not to favor any country in which they do business over any other such country. The logical extension of this view is the irrelevance of territoriality and nation-state boundaries.

> "For business purposes," says the president of the IBM World Trade Corporation, "the boundaries that separate one nation from another are no more real than the equator. They are merely convenient demarcations of ethnic, linguistic, and cultural entities. They do not define business requirements or consumer trends. Once management understands and accepts this world economy, its view of the marketplace—and its planning—necessarily expand. The world outside the home country is no longer viewed as a series of disconnected customers and prospects for its products, but as an extension of a single market." (Barnet and Muller 1974, 14–15)

These issues, now frequently raised by economists and students of international business as well as political scientists engaged in international political economy, return us to a question that has been at the heart of numerous theoretical (and methodological) debates in the study of international relations—the continuing relevance of the sovereign state in both the practice and the analysis of world politics. This question strikes at the core issues of international relations: the nature of the international system, the nature of the key components of that system, and the question of change in the international system. As noted earlier, this question again considers how states (and other international actors) adapt to their changing environments.

Using the basic conceptual building blocks briefly presented in Part 1, I will outline a few possible responses to this most recent set of challenges to the centrality of the state. Within the context of Part 1, it should also be no surprise that I both agree and disagree with the central arguments of the economics-based positions of this particular group of transnationally oriented scholars. While I agree with the notion that interdependence has affected, and continues to affect, the workings of the formally anarchic Westphalian state system including the nature of state sovereignty, I disagree with the manner in which some of the key questions have been formulated as well as with a number of the conclusions reached.

That is, while we have been pointed in essentially the correct direction, I think there are flaws in some of the basic assumptions and how the issues have been structured and characterized. Rather than look at the either-or proposition that transnational forces (in whatever form) diminish the state, or that the growth of interdependence (in whatever form) *must* reduce the relevance of the state, I prefer to see the issue as the coexistence of states and transnational forces (the statecentric and multicentric systems, as argued by Rosenau 1990). Instead, following our central concern, the key question should be "how to manage interdependence" in a world of both states and a variety of nonstate, transnational actors. While chapter 6 will use a discussion of international law and organization as it derives from Part 1 to critique Realism, the present chapter critiques at least one form of the transnational perspective. I argue that in *both cases* there is a lack of appreciation of the basic nature of the international system, how states react and adapt to that system, and—most important—the complex feedback processes that exist between the state units or entities and the systemic environment.

Challenging the continued centrality of the state has an extensive and honorable history. For example, John Herz (1957) predicted the demise of the territorial state because it could no longer provide the protection that, he argued, had been the basis for the selection of different forms of human organization. The territorial state, he proposed, would be replaced by the "bloc," a much larger mode of organization, dominated by a single power, and the only form of organization capable of existing in a bipolar world of nuclear superpowers. Herz, it should be remembered, had also popularized the concept of the security dilemma. Both the security dilemma and the meta-Prisoner's Dilemma indicate that there was a powerful security interdependence in the international system. The security dilemma indicated how the quest for security could generate externalities—and how "order" as a collective good required mechanisms to manage collective action.

Yet, as a good Realist who saw the only effective system regulator as some form of the balance of power, Herz was concerned with how—and in what form—the balancing regulator could work in a world of strategic nuclear weapons. Herz argued that the strategic interdependence of states (which could no longer maintain a "hard shell" against the penetration of nuclear delivery systems) would lead to the demise of the territorial state and lead to the emergence of blocs as the central actors.

A decade later Herz (1968) recanted. He recognized that the allure and power of the territorial state as a mode of organization transcended his earlier argument regarding defense, to issues of identity, recognition, and status. Indeed, smaller and smaller units had been clamoring for the establishment of independent states of their own—to permit them a legitimate institutional basis for interacting in the global system. We see, paradoxically, a more vigorous version of this argument in Rosenau's 1990 discussion of the fragmentation of contemporary states into smaller separatist units (each unit, however, desiring to establish a new state of its own).

In Rosenau's presentation, turbulence is characterized by the disruption of regularities, where "environments are marked by high degrees of complexity and dynamism" (1990, 9). One of the primary sources of global turbulence and change are processes of *decentralization,* what Rosenau calls "subgroupism." This tendency takes many forms. One is the emergence of former long-established "microstates" into full membership in the state system through admission to the UN (e.g., Liechtenstein in 1990, San Marino in 1992, and Andorra and Monaco in 1993). A second source of global turbulence and change has been the breakup of multiethnic states or empires, such as the former Soviet Union and the former Yugoslavia, as well as the division of Czechoslovakia. Since 1990, eighteen new members of the UN have been the products of fragmentation, with an additional half dozen the result of microstate entry.

The System, the State, and *Sovereignty*

The durability of the state, even as its hard shell disappears and the security-based argument for its existence loses its relevance, also brings into question commentary by *both* Realists and transnationalists regarding territoriality. In a similar manner, both perspectives make territoriality *the* defining characteristic of the sovereign state, rather than as but one part of a more complex concept. We must look briefly at the state system and the formal aspects of the state and sovereignty to get at least a fundamental understanding of this more complex concept.

European history before the rise of states reflected the politics and interactions of cultures, religion, and individual nobles or princes more than of states. A convergence of political, economic, technological, and religious factors that began in Europe around 1000 A.D. helped create the state, replacing personal and societal bonds with international relations. And again, all the factors were related in complex feedback loops; each affected every other and was in turn affected by the results of earlier processes.[2] Tilly (1990) in his study of the rise of the Western national state focuses on two central elements: capital and coercion. As monarchs attempted to expand, centralize, and consolidate their control over territory and people in their struggles against the feudal nobility, they needed wealth and resources (capital) and the means to prosecute war (coercion). These factors provided the opportunities that enabled kings to engage in this process and ultimately to succeed against the nobles.

Thus, one way to begin to define the state is to see it, as does Tilly, as an entity that expanded to control and govern multiple contiguous regions and their cities. The state resulted from activities related to coercion and to the control of goods and services. Coercion included war, to defeat external rivals, and state making, to defeat internal rivals. Here Tilly brings in both the external and internal components of sovereignty to be discussed subsequently.

The split in Christendom and the religious wars that followed provided the final element needed to connect the political, economic, and technological factors that had been developing. These religious wars dominated the history of the sixteenth century and the early seventeenth, culminating in the Thirty Years' War, which ended with the Treaty of Westphalia in 1648. They were the last factor in the creation of the sovereign state.

The central principle of the Treaty of Westphalia was apparently simple: the ruler of a territory would determine the religion of that territory. This principle had been articulated as early as the Peace of Augsburg in 1555. Despite its simplicity, this principle had enormous consequences: the major internal issue of the day—religion—was to be determined by the ruler, not by an external authority, whether the Holy Roman Emperor or the pope. No longer was there even the pretense of religious or political unity in Europe. Authority was dispersed to the various kings and princes, and the basis for the sovereign state was established. On each territory there were no longer multiple loyalties and authorities; there was only one: loyalty to the authority of the king or prince. The territory and the people on that territory belonged to the ruler, who did not have to answer to an external authority. Thus the Westphalian state system distinguished itself not only from the feudal principle, but also from the basic imperial or hegemonic principle of the suzerainty of a higher authority that existed

---

2. This discussion draws upon the work of Bull (1977), Tilly (1975, 1990), McNeill (1982), Bull and Watson (1984), and Mann (1988).

elsewhere across the globe at that time—in India, China, the Arab Islamic world, and the Mongol-Tatar system.

Thus, territoriality *is* important. However, the full impact of territoriality could not be realized without the government and the state—that is, sovereignty. The government must be conceived as the agent of the state. The state must be considered a *legal* entity having the special status of sovereignty. The very term *state,* which arose in the sixteenth century, derived from the Latin *status,* which meant the "position" or "standing" of a ruler. The state is thus a legal entity; it has been invested with a legal status and a legal equality with all other states that have been denied all other actors on the international or global scene. Like a corporation, the state has no concrete existence; it is a legal abstraction. Through its government and the representatives of that government, the state undertakes legal commitments, both rights and responsibilities (e.g., signing treaties or joining organizations). We should understand, then, that sovereignty can also act to constrain states as well as give them special status (as Rosenau noted, they are "sovereignty-bound" and in some situations they may have less freedom of action than some "sovereignty-free" nonstate actors).

Sovereignty should be seen as indicating a special, theoretical relationship between each state and all other states. Bull (1977, 8) noted that sovereignty includes "internal sovereignty, which means supremacy over all other authorities within that territory and population," and "external sovereignty, by which is meant not supremacy but independence of outside authorities. The sovereignty of states, both internal and external, may be said to exist both at a normative level and at a factual level." Thus sovereignty has an ideal meaning that in principle gives states an equal legal status. A sovereign state has complete control over the people and territory represented by its government. Ideally, it also means that there is external autonomy: no authority exists to order the state how to act; there is no actor with the legitimate authority to tell a state what to do.

Note that this external autonomy is the essence of the "anarchic" international system—the same anarchic system that creates the security dilemma and the meta-Prisoner's Dilemma. It should now be clear how the central theme of this chapter reflects the central theme of this book: the history of the interaction of sovereign states is their attempt to develop and employ regulatory mechanisms by which they could create order, manage externalities, and control conflict within this anarchic environment.

Transnational Challenges to Statecentric Models

Arguments about the irrelevance of territorial-based state units thus share one problem with Realism—the exaggeration of territoriality in conceptualizing the Westphalian state. However, the irrelevance of territorial state actors argument also shares a number of assumptions—and problems—with transnationalism. Here we use transnationalism to cover the whole range of theories or models or perspectives of how to think about international relations or world politics that have challenged the Realist view of international relations. Many of these transnational challenges to Realist models specifically question the Realist assumption that the sovereign state is the only actor of consequence in world politics. They additionally challenge the assumption that the security of the state, as measured by military capability, dominates the agenda of all states in the anarchic Westphalian system.

Various models of transnational relations derive from, or are reflected in, the work of Keohane and Nye (1972, 1989). Keohane and Nye's formulation of "complex interdependence,"[3] which was briefly outlined in chapter 2, refutes the notion that only states count. It argues that there are numerous other consequential actors and interactions, that there no longer exists a set hierarchy of issues dominated by the concerns of military security, and that complex interdependence precludes the use of military force among a number of states (1989, 24–25).

In this formulation we find some basic arguments as to how interdependence constrains the behavior of sovereign states, yet in no way does it argue that sovereignty or territoriality have become irrelevant. Keohane and Nye introduce a theme that Rosenau (1990) subsequently takes much further: that important consequences flow from the behavior of nonstate actors, which include international or intergovernmental organizations, nongovernmental organizations, "transgovernmental organizations" (the interactions and transactions of governmental bureaus and offices across states, without the knowledge or approval of high-level governmental decision makers), and even individuals. All these other nonstate actors, *because* they exist within an interdependent system, are able to affect the other actors in the system, even the most "powerful" states. Because entities within an interdependent system are sensitive and vulnerable to each other, even the smallest can produce significant outcomes on some issues at some times—this ability is what we earlier called "behavioral power," following Ward and House (1988). It is crucial to note, however, that an argument proposing the existence of other consequential actors is quite different from arguing that territorial states are no longer important, are becoming irrelevant, or are in the process of disappearing.

---

3. I think this is an unfortunate term because it erroneously conflates the phenomenon of systemic interdependence based on externalities, with the specific substance of non-Realist strategies, behavior, and ways of viewing the arena of global politics. Better labels would be "transnational interdependence" or a model of "interdependent transnational linkages."

A number of transnationalist writings fall into this trap, foreseeing an international system where transnationalist forces bring about some sort of evolutionary change in the nature of the territorial, sovereign state. Rosenau (1990), on the other hand, claims that a multicentric system of "sovereignty-free" actors has grown up alongside a statecentric system composed of "sovereignty-bound" actors. Although there have been critiques of Rosenau's side-by-side conception, preferring instead to see the two systems integrated in a multilayered structure (e.g., Kuhlman 1997), Rosenau's key argument stands: that the statecentric system exists, will continue to exist, and will continue to have important affects on nonstate actors. Despite his massive evidence demonstrating the existence and importance of the multicentric system, and powerful transnational forces,[4] Rosenau is not arguing that such phenomena demonstrate an evolutionary process eventuating in the disappearance of the state.

Rosenau's work supports Keohane and Nye's complex interdependence framework and its arguments linking power and interdependence. States continue to exist and even are "powerful" in certain contexts and under certain conditions. However, nonstate actors, not constrained or bound by sovereignty (which imposes responsibilities as well as rights) may be more "powerful" than states in other situations: power is relational and contextual, and the military capabilities of states are *not* fungible across issues. Baldwin (1989, 133–34) has presented persuasive arguments that "[w]hat functions as a power resource in one policy-contingency framework may be irrelevant in another." In addition, political power resources—especially military capabilities—"tend to be much less liquid than economic resources . . . [with] no standardized measure of value that serves as a medium of exchange for political power resources" (134). While Baldwin attributes to IR scholars the "tendency to exaggerate the fungibility of power resources, often to the point of ignoring scope and domain" (138), I think the charge is more appropriately leveled at Realists.

Realists not only exaggerate the fungibility of military power—and thus overvalue the military power of states vis-à-vis other actors—they ignore the profoundly different forms "power" may take. Hart (1976) has conceptualized power as three forms of "control"—control over resources, actors, and outcomes. Realist analyses focus predominantly on power simply as control over resources. Power can take many shapes as control over actors and control over outcomes, however. In addition, as control over actors and outcomes, power in any of these forms *is not zero sum.* Thus, the ability of other types of actors to wield influence does not

---

4. Which includes all the transactions and linkages that constitute and indicate the emergence of international integration.

mean states are no longer able to do so. It only means that there are many other forms of influence and that these other forms of influence derive from many different types of capabilities (those that can affect sensitivity and vulnerability).

How is power to be managed under conditions of interdependence? Not necessarily by states using military force. Thus, we have the second component of complex interdependence:

> The agenda of interstate relationships consists of multiple issues that are not arranged in a clear or consistent hierarchy. This *absence of hierarchy among issues* means, among other things, that military security does not consistently dominate the agenda. Many issues arise from what used to be considered domestic policy, and the distinction between domestic and foreign issues becomes blurred. (Keohane and Nye 1989, 25, emphasis in original)

The third element of complex interdependence concerns the nonuse of force by states. It rests on the social-communication integration theory of Deutsch et al. (1957) and the Deutschian concept of security community, which is the product of social integration. Increased transactions between societies at a variety of levels (and thus including transnational relations that bypass the high-level interaction of governmental leaders) produce responsiveness and feelings of community, which derive from the mutual gain brought about by increased interdependence. By definition, integration is the process by which increasing interdependence is managed in a positive way—without exploitation, with gains to all parties, and with the expectation of compliance to the demands and needs of the other parties *without* even considering the option of military force or the threat of force.[5]

It should be clear, then, that integration theory and research challenge several of the basic assumptions necessary for Realism on both the theoretical and the behavioral level (see Puchala 1981 and Lijphart 1981). Integration theory and research challenge the idea that states are in a constant "struggle" for power and military security because of the nature of the anarchic system that generates the need for self-help. Integration the-

---

5. Note that the core of the security community concept is the absence of even the consideration of the use of military force. This focus on the development of norms against the use of force, norms that erase even the thought of the option of force, is the central argument presented in Mueller's 1989 work arguing for the obsolescence of war. While the "democratic peace" will be discussed in chapter 7, here it is important to draw the reader's attention to the similarities between the Deutschian security community and Boulding's (1978) "stable peace," as well as Singer and Wildavsky's (1993) "zones of peace."

ory and research challenge the idea that war is thus the ultimate recourse among states. Yet, even with such powerful challenges as these to Realism, integration theory and research *do not* challenge the existence of and sovereignty of states. States manage interdependence through the creation of security communities.

Importantly, Deutsch indicates that while there have been amalgamated security communities, where states integrate fully into a new state (e.g. the Swiss cantons), security communities may also be "pluralistic." That means that states need not give up independence or territorial integrity to achieve significant levels of integration or to benefit from the positive processes that are possible with interdependence. While we shall look at "Expected-Utility and Integration" in chapter 7, it is important to note here that there may be no rational, cost-benefit reason for states to move beyond pluralistic security communities to amalgamated ones. If pluralistic security communities can bring peace and security, as well as foster overall economic growth and well-being, it would be "rational" for policymakers to avoid the heavy costs of amalgamation and be content with the substantial benefits found in this pluralistic product of integration. Ernst Haas and students, pessimistic over the apparent lack of movement toward a single European state, prematurely declared European integration at an end, along with their efforts to study it. The Haasians erroneously looked only at the end product of integration and not its continuing processes.[6]

Therefore, it is clearly possible for territorial boundaries, sovereign claims to equality, independence, and consent *to coexist* with high levels of interdependence and transnational activities. The supranational character of various European Union IGOs does point to the possibility of a systematic reduction of the sovereignty of EU members. Yet, member interactions such as those accompanying the debate and resolution of the European Monetary System issue (with Britain retaining the sovereign element of consent through the option not to join) continue to demonstrate the coexistence of integration and sovereignty.

In brief, a closer look at the nature of interdependence and transnationalism, power, and integration indicates that greater movements toward transnational activities—and even integration—*do not necessarily* indicate the demise of the territorial state or even a significant diminution of its formal or legal sovereignty.

---

6. Caporaso and Keller (1993, 15) note that "while these rough measures of political and economic integration manifest integrative stagnation during the EEC 'dark age,' they do not manifest the sort of precipitous disintegration that Haas and others once thought possible."

States, Context, and Environment: How Does a or the System Work?

At the risk of oversimplification, recall that one economic transnationalist argument is that the territorial state is becoming outmoded because territoriality and sovereignty imply borders, and that borders are made inconsequential by the transnational integration of markets. For example, Kobrin's 1997 chapter subhead "National Markets under Fire" translates into "Territorial States under Fire." Here, again, Kobrin is basically asking whether or not borders remain relevant. Similarly, Nigh (1997) asks "what will home and host country mean?" Nigh thus raises Robert Reich's (1990, 1991) questions—"Who is Us?" and "Who is Them?" In this section I wish to come at "how to manage interdependence?" from another angle, questioning the interpretation of system and borders implicit in the transnational economics position and arguing that the ideas of "national markets" or national economies are at least "quasi myths."[7]

Let us begin by returning to some observations about systems in general and then the international system as one type of social system. Only in this way can we understand the *inherent* tension between the concept of the sovereign state and the interdependence within which states have existed for five hundred years. We need to keep in mind the Sprouts' ecological triad of entity, environment, and the entity-environment relationship. The entity-environment relationship is concerned in part with how environments affect the opportunities afforded to entities, as well as how they affect the willingness of decision makers in those entities to make choices. These relationships are not deterministic. Recall that while environments provide possibilities and help set probabilities, they must be perceived by decision makers.

All systems, by definition, are composed of interacting elements. Their interactions are characterized by interdependence—the sensitivity and vulnerability of the elements toward each other. The elements of a system have a structure: they can be arrayed along various hierarchies according to their attributes—for example, military capabilities, economic wealth, status, or prestige. Patterns of their interactions can be discerned. In their concern with system stability, various analysts—such as Rose-

---

7. In a critique of the "Who is US" thesis presented by Reich, Kapstein (1991, 56) argues, "The power of the home state over the multinational has not diminished; if anything, it has continued to increase. Corporations have not become anational, multinational, or transnational; they remain wedded to their home governments for both political and economic reasons. The question 'Who is US?' is an interesting one, but it is not asked by business executives."

crance—have discussed the consequences of disturbances within systems and how such disturbances are handled.

The feudal condition that existed in Europe following the disintegration of the Roman Empire was, in part, characterized by both the local organization of political authority and local economy. As addressed earlier, the development and interaction of the political, military, technological, economic, and religious factors that eventuated in the rise of statelike actors also increased the size and interaction between these entities (for a brief overview, see Russett and Starr 1996, chap. 3; also Tilly 1990). That is, groups of entities that exhibited only the most rudimentary elements of a system were increasing the interactions and interdependencies that would create a true system.

In the formative stages, from around 1100 to 1648 (the nominal beginning of the modern state system and the date of the Peace of Westphalia), this system developed a supposedly dual hierarchical structure: (1) a political or temporal structure based on feudalism and the hierarchy of loyalty that hypothetically culminated with the Holy Roman Emperor, and (2) a spiritual structure that was based on the hierarchy established by the Catholic Church (along with what Michael McGinnis has termed "ideological interdependence"). In Rosecrance's terms, the same hierarchies that helped structure the system also worked as systemic regulators to resolve conflicts and handle other demands and disturbances.

The establishment of the Westphalian state system threw off these two centers of authority. The distinction of this new system, states with "sovereignty," was that the units in the system were each ruled by a prince for whom no legitimate source of higher external authority existed. Thus, from the *beginning* of the Westphalian system, the state actors *were* in a system—by definition they were linked by various types of economic-commercial, military, political, and social interdependencies. Because they were interdependent units in a system without a formal central authority, the states needed to develop new types of regulators so that they could prosper, could do what they needed to do, could get what they needed from each other. These are the feedback loops between disturbance and regulator, between problems and the mechanisms to create solutions, which were detailed in chapters 3 and 4.

The development of mechanisms such as international law to facilitate the interactions of the states, as well as informal sanctioning mechanisms such as the balance of power, indicate that the states *were indeed in an interdependent system* that required regulating mechanisms. The growth of states depended in large part on the growth of commerce and its need to expand ever outward as well as the way in which commerce linked separate political entities in interdependent networks. Erstwhile European monarchs used the dynamism of commerce to obtain the wealth and capital needed to defeat the nobles, consolidate their rule, and create areas of internal order (Tilly's "capital"), despite the fact that commerce always put them into contact with others and was hard to "control." McNeill (1982) persuasively argues that it was the opposition to commerce (and all it entailed, including the necessary linkages and interdependencies) that led to the stagnation of imperial China. Both McNeill and Kennedy (1987) demonstrate that China had the potential to outstrip the formative European system in the 1400s and 1500s but failed to do so.

Gilpin (1987, 10–11) clearly delineates the tension that has *always* existed between states and markets:

> On the one hand, the state is based on the concepts of territoriality, loyalty and exclusivity, and it possesses a monopoly on the legitimate use of force. Although no state can long survive unless it assures the interests and gains the consent of the most powerful groups in society, states enjoy varying degrees of autonomy with respect to the societies of which they are a part. On the other hand the market is based on the concepts of functional integration, contractual relationships, and expanding interdependence of buyers and sellers . . . For the states, territorial boundaries are a necessary basis of national autonomy and political unity. For the market, the elimination of all political and other obstacles to the operation of the price mechanism is imperative. The tension between these two fundamentally different ways of ordering human relationships has profoundly shaped the course of modern history and constitutes the crucial problem in the study of political economy.

This long citation supports one of the basic premises of economics transnationalists, the tension that exists between territorially defined states and transnational markets. However, Gilpin's observations also indicate that markets have always linked states, and states have always had to manage the interdependence generated by commerce.[8]

The idea that "national" markets or economies at some point in time stood separate from systemic interdependencies is untenable (somewhat like Hobbes's "state of nature"). From the beginning, states were interde-

---

8. Among the vast literature on political economy, two useful reviews of the relationships between economics and politics or states and markets are Caporaso and Levine 1992 and Schwartz 1994. Schwartz is particularly good at presenting the feedback loop between economics and politics in his discussion of "how markets created distinct spatial patterns in what was produced and how states attempted to influence that distribution of production" (1994, 6).

pendent. Their notion of sovereignty had to deal with the externalities of sensitivity and vulnerability. Rather than note how interdependence erodes sovereignty, the question is that posed in the title of this book: how have states managed interdependence at different points in time under different conditions? There has always been a tension between markets and sovereignty, between economics and politics.

The "Westphalian Trade-Off" Revisited

Returning to the Sprouts' ecological triad and the ideas of opportunity and willingness, we have an alternative way to look at the relationship between sovereignty and interdependence. A state can be seen as an entity that exists within an environment. This environment sets the "menu for choice" for the decision makers of the state. The decision makers are nested within a set of environments, each of which provides possibilities or opportunities as well as providing cues that affect the probability of choice, or willingness. Interdependence is a significant component of this environment, with the possibilities and probabilities of state choice shaped by its externalities. The question is: How do states adapt themselves to their environments? Which parts of these environments produce sensitivities to which states are most vulnerable? How are these to be managed or handled?

In the same way Rosenau's multicentric system of nonstate, sovereignty-free transnational actors also forms part of the environment of the territorial state, states must react and adapt to the constraints that such actors and actions place on them as well. The mechanisms for dealing with system demands and disturbances change with the change in system structure, especially the distribution of resources (economic or military). For example, the main regulatory mechanism of the post–1945 period until the mid-1980s was the strategic balance of terror between the superpowers. This regulatory mechanism was one version of the balance-of-power process, that is, a deterrence process. It usefully regulated not only the conflict behavior between superpowers, but between the allies of each. Within large blocs of states, order was kept by superpowers. Outside the blocs, because there were *two* superpowers, the system provided the possibility of support against whichever superpower attempted influence, and thus the possibility of superpower conflict and the possibility of the escalation of that conflict. Therefore, the superpower balance actually permeated into all areas of systemic order.

With the disappearance of one of the superpowers, the system structure and the possibilities it provided have changed; there is a different

menu facing decision makers.[9] There is also the need for regulatory mechanisms to take the place of the balance of terror. An incipient "new world
order," which is simply the traditional notion of collective security, is seen
by some as a way to manage world security order. In the same way, the end
of World War II brought about not only a capitalist world economic system, but a supposedly alternative economic system of socialist states.
Within the context of the cold war, the Western economic system required
regulatory mechanisms. Western states produced a network of formal and
informal rules, norms, and patterns of behavior along with IGOs to deal
with many economic issues—that is, regimes.

The evolution of regimelike mechanisms to deal with mutual problems, interdependent linkages, externalities, and collective goods indicates
how states adapt to their environments. Rather than the state-to-state military treaties of the nineteenth century to deal with strategic interdependences, the post-1945 regimes dealt primarily with economic issues and
explicitly included nonstate actors in attempts to manage the coordination
needs of some regimes and the more difficult cooperation needs of other
regimes (see Stein 1983; Keohane 1984). To continue, the whole literature
dealing with the role of hegemonic leadership in the creation and maintenance of regimes is about *changing conditions* and how mechanisms created to regulate the system and help maintain order are affected by change;
how they are modified to deal with change.

In sum, different issues and problems, involving different mixes of
collective and private goods, call for different modes of organization and
regulatory mechanisms. The formally anarchic condition of the international system makes this process more complex. However, such has *always*
been the case. Many of the attempts to adapt to and deal with growing
interdependences since 1945 have indicated the degree of flexibility possible without centralized authority or guidance.

One of the advantages of central authority is having a mechanism for
clearly delineating rights and responsibilities among the members of the
system—who is expected to do what or for whom under what conditions.
As noted, such mechanisms are in place to allow a system to function
smoothly, to facilitate the interactions of the constituent units and permit
them to do what they need to do. Yet, the international system—one without central authority—does indeed have similar mechanisms. The oldest

---

9. And note that this momentous change in the political and military character of the
system—certainly consonant with any of the historical system changes outlined by Rosecrance—occurred *without* a general systemic war between the system hegemon and its primary challenger.

such mechanism is international law, which shall be investigated in the following chapter—as part of a critique of Realism.

One of the purposes of the concept of sovereignty—an abstract legal condition that characterizes states—was to delineate as clearly as possible in a decentralized system who was responsible for what (the notion of jurisdiction over people and territory). The development of international law served the same purpose of delineating rights and responsibilities. Every form of interdependence made this process less clear and more difficult, yet *more necessary*. With ecological externalities, the territorial demarcation of states loses much of its meaning for some purposes. However, the territorial boundaries still indicate which government is responsible for what behavior of which people where.

In this sense, the questions raised about the national origin of products, about whether an IBM notebook is an American or Japanese product, are not necessarily the correct set of questions if one is questioning the continued relevance of the territorial state. The territorial state retains relevance *because* these "us" and "them" questions concern legal issues of jurisdiction and responsibility for impeding or facilitating trade. Such questions of coordination or control (e.g., the origin and control of technology) are dealt with by states, international law, and regimes. They are dealt with through bargaining, whether bilateral diplomatic contacts or the forums provided by IGOs that exist or are created to deal with a specific functional issue (as is central to the regime literature). This point is illustrated by the comments of Kapstein (1991, 56), who notes that

> In general, large corporations are not only aware of the identity of their home country, they wish to maintain a close relationship with the government. Only the state can defend corporate interests in international negotiations over trade, investment, and market access. Agreements over such things as airline routes, the opening of banking establishments, and the right to sell insurance are not decided by corporate actors who gather around a table; they are determined by diplomats and bureaucrats.

It is fair to ask at what point systems (or any organization) can no longer adapt to their environments; when the organization or structure of the system is dysfunctional for such adaptation. Has a system composed of sovereign territorial states reached such a point? One reason for discussing the work of Herz was to indicate that the territorial state continued to thrive even when the territorial aspect of security was no longer relevant to state survival. Sovereignty provided other benefits—of status, prestige, and entry into the arena of global politics, with the benefits of legal equality and autonomy. Sovereignty as a legal concept also helps identify rights and responsibilities as just noted. The discussion of integration and Deutschian security communities also serves to indicate that high levels of interdependence can connect states through a variety of transnational linkages but *not* lead to the disappearance of the state or even a significant alteration in its organization in order to adapt to changing conditions.

The adaptation of the state to growing networks of interdependence has indeed led to a shift in the balance of the "Westphalian trade-off"— between interdependence and the autonomy/independence/nonintervention in domestic-affairs aspects of sovereignty (discussed in chapter 2).

While economics transnationalists have identified some of the forces that have been responsible for the trade-off, they are wrong about the consequences. In adapting to an evolving menu for choice, the leaders of states have developed regulatory mechanisms that are seen to be useful for dealing with contemporary interdependences—working through IGOs or NGOs and learning how to craft bargains in situations where interdependence predominates (e.g., see Keohane and Nye 1989) and where state relations are defined within pluralistic security communities. Just as we will turn next to international law, we will return to security communities in chapter 7.

CHAPTER 6

International Law: Creating Order in the Westphalian System

Several themes have emerged in the discussion so far—the relationship between entity and environment, the necessity for states to adapt to changing environments, what factors create special needs and conditions that make adaptation both more difficult and more crucial. The context shaped by interdependence and externalities has continually created such needs, and states have responded with different types of system "regulators." My aim in this chapter is to outline a scheme by which we could think theoretically about one such regulator: international law. Though it is a long-standing (perhaps even *initial*) feature of interstate relations, it is not apparent that international relations scholars have a clear understanding of international law's role in the international system, or how it both reflects and contributes to order and "society" in that system.

While this chapter will primarily be a critique of Realist approaches, I will also attempt to distinguish (and then partially reconcile) Realist and non–Realist/Idealist/"Neoliberal" conceptions of international law. I will do so by first looking at the general relationship between law and "order" and then at the more specific relationship between international law and international society. Next, I will outline Realist and Liberal—or Grotian, in Bull's (1977) terms—views of international law as law, and then look at the functions of law in the anarchic society by stressing the interdependent nature of the international system. Finally, international law will be viewed as a mechanism for global order under changing conditions of interdependence. Realist and neoliberal responses to the question "how to manage interdependence?" will then provide a perspective that can be used in to reconcile some aspects of these contending views of international law.

International Law and the Westphalian State System

Definitions of international law stress that it is composed of a body of *rules* that somehow governs states in their relations and that it delineates both the rights and the obligations of states in these relations. A typical example is given by Bull (1977, 127): "International law may be regarded as a body of rules which binds states and other agents in world politics in their relations with one another and is considered to have the status of law." Key questions that are raised by such definitions concern *how* states that are sovereign, existing within the formally anarchic Westphalian system, can be "bound" by some "law" that has not been generated, is not interpreted, and cannot be enforced by a centralized, legitimate authority.

Such questions are really concerned with where law comes from, the nature of such law and thus on what basis such rules are binding, and why the subjects of international law would obey "law." These questions also highlight the central idea that law can only take on meaning given the context of the system or "society" within which it is supposed to operate; that system or society in turn is shaped by the meanings attached by its units to its essential concepts (i.e., "states," "sovereignty," and "anarchy").

Broadly, two approaches to law traditionally have been argued. Taking the first, law may be based on transcendent, universalistic principles—they apply to all people at all times under all circumstances. The basis for obligation in this natural law perspective derives from the existence of universal principles (whether derived from divine sources or general laws such as those of the natural sciences that apply to all of nature) that are "self-evident to any individual exercising his 'right reason,' or the moral faculty with which he was endowed" (von Glahn 1992, 26).

Alternatively, positivist theories of law maintain that law is what people say is law. The basis for obligation derives from self-interest, utility, and consent. The binding nature of rules comes from customary behavior, that is, the regularized and predictable practices of those who created the rules. Custom includes the articulation of expectations about rights and obligations (*opinio juris*). This view of international law corresponded well with concepts of the "social contract" as argued by such writers as Vattel in the eighteenth century, and it was particularly well suited to the nineteenth-century liberal utilitarianism of Mill and Bentham.

The dominant view of international law, as presented in contemporary international law and international relations texts, is positivist. However, the existence of an "eclectic" approach, which has attempted to combine the two by adding natural law to the self-interest and consent core of positivism, as found in the international law of human rights, should be noted. The positivist approach—that international law is what the subjects of international law agree the law is—has important consequences. It means that international law, as Hoffmann's "mirror," will reflect the *degree* of society in the international system in terms of what states find it in their interest to consent to and the degree of consensus that emerges. It reflects the various factors that lead states (and other actors) to obey international law; the conditions under which states find themselves constrained by international law, even if that constraint is self-constraint.

Charles Kegley (1995) in the introductory essay of an edited volume that presents the "neoliberal challenge" to Realism, notes that we must be concerned with "factors that promote change and continuity," that "circumstance and context also matter"; Goertz (1994) investigates "context as changing meaning." The positivist view of international law drives us to consider the same assumption—that law is situational and reflects evolving politics, political structures, and dynamics of the system at some specific time in history. Again, the consequences of a positivist view of international law may be summarized for introductory purposes by returning to Hoffmann's view that international law is a magnifying mirror, which reflects world politics. This view leads to a perspective on international law that falls somewhere between the two extreme views held by international relations scholars: that international law has no impact on the activities of states, and that international law can solve all our global problems.

Kegley (1995) also entreats scholars involved in the search for theoretical perspectives for the study of international relations to ask, "What is new? What is constant?" As was central to the arguments of the previous chapter, which critiqued certain transnational approaches, the reflecting-mirror view of international law stresses certain *constants*. Several constants have been discussed so far. One is that international law is part of the environment or context of states. International law comprises one part of the set of "opportunities" and constraints within which states must act. In one of many feedback loops we have proposed, the society of states in the international system creates law, but that law in turn becomes part of the context within which the society of states and its individual members must act, constraining them through a set of rules that alters the incentives, costs, and benefits of various possible choices and behaviors.

A second constant is the tension between the anarchy of the Westphalian system and the need for order—the Westphalian trade-off. As noted, the Westphalian trade-off stressed independence and autonomy, as against the lack of order inherent in the formal anarchy of a system of "sovereign" states. Yet, as argued in the previous chapter, even then it was an international *system*. And, for any system to exist, these interactions must also entail some degree of interdependence: events and changes in one part of the system inevitably will have effects and consequences in other parts (sensitivity and vulnerability).

Thus, the international system, as any system, must deal with all the problems and opportunities generated by interdependence and, since Westphalia, must do so within the constraints of a formally anarchic structure. States find themselves facing a reality consisting of both interdependence and anarchy. International anarchy, according to Kenneth Waltz (1959), consists of many sovereign states, with no system of law enforceable by centralized authorities, thus generating a reliance on self-help, and with *each* state the "final judge of its own cause."

Bull (1977), while apparently recognizing the realities of both anarchy and interdependence, argues that the international system additionally reflects a "society" of states. From this argument derives the basic Grotian or Liberal view of international law and international politics. All units in social life, existing within some society (which must be the case for units of people existing in an interdependent system), are seen to have three primary or elementary goals: security against violence, assurance that agreements will be kept, and stability of possession or ownership. Meeting such goals will bring about *order* within a social system.[1]

Rosecrance's systemic "regulators" are the mechanisms used to deal with disturbances within the system, with the demands of its units, and with the set of problems that *ultimately reduce* to Bull's three basic components of order. As developed earlier, through a complex set of economic, political, technological, and religious factors a system of states arose, each of which was endowed with a special legal status—sovereignty. In so doing, the states had thrown off a set of putative regulatory mechanisms consisting of the spiritual hierarchy of the Catholic Church and the temporal hierarchy of feudalism culminating in the Holy Roman Emperor.

New regulatory mechanisms were needed. With a system of sovereign states to replace a vertical system of centralized authority, such mechanisms would, of necessity, be informal. Realists have stressed the balance of power as the informal mechanism most relevant to achieving and maintaining order in the Westphalian system and have dismissed (or, at the least, *undervalued*) the regulatory capacity of a system of law that lacked centralized, authoritative enforcement capabilities.

In contrast, the Liberal view gave international law a more prominent place in regulating order. Here is where one of our central feedback loops emerges. The special condition of sovereignty created new conditions and requirements for regulatory mechanisms. It fostered the emergence of a

---

1. Note that this view does not automatically equate any social system with "society"—social units may be interdependent along a number of dimensions and yet have no mutually recognized expectations or rules. My interpretation of what Bull argues is that the social units called states have *always* had some level of agreed expectations about order, have *always* recognized their need to interact and the need to constrain those interactions. Thus, the social system of sovereign states has always had some level of society; the Hobbesian "state of nature" is fiction, not a representation of history.

system of rules and laws that could deal with the needs of states and which reflected the self-interests and consent (sovereignty!) of those states. Such laws in turn reinforced and further developed the concept of sovereignty as the legal basis for states and for the expansion of state power and control. States, needing mechanisms for order, created norms and rules—law— that permitted states to do what they wanted to do, to do so more efficiently and in such ways as to enhance the status of states.

The three basic elements of order presented by Bull indicate that order entails, at essence, the avoidance of chaos, capriciousness, and unpredictability. Patterns of activities that permit some degree of certainty and predictability, that rest on expectations of how others (and oneself) are supposed to behave, constitute *order.* Norms specify rules that make for predictability: they delineate boundaries, they serve as signposts for behavior, they routinize relations, they serve as a trip wire to focus attention on violations of expectations (see Kegley and Raymond 1990). Such consequences of norms are central to Bull's thesis. Because of the existence and impact of norms, order can exist either without formal, written rules or with only rudimentary rules.[2] To Bull, order is the basis of any society. Given this definition of order, society can then exist *without* formal rules. Hence, there is not only an international system, but also an international "society" because there is an order based on sets of expectations of behavior and repetitive patterns of behavior. This order is encompassed not only in treaties and written international law, but in the informal norms of customary international law.[3]

I have tried to establish several points relevant to this section. There are certain constants that Realists (as well as Liberals/Neoliberals or transnationalists) need to recognize. As a *system* of states, the international system has *always* needed regulatory mechanisms to foster order among its interdependent component units. I have tried briefly to indicate that international order—which implies an international society—can exist without a centralized authority or legal system and that order does

---

2. International law has been characterized by various scholars as a system of law that is primitive, incomplete, decentralized, or imperfect. See also Barkun 1968.

3. Recent studies have demonstrated the powerful impact of norms (what Gary Goertz and Paul Diehl [1992] call "decentralized norms") on the behavior of sovereign states in the formally anarchic international system. Changes in expectations of how states ought to behave, along with an understanding of the benefits to self-interest that exist through self-constraint and compliance, have occurred in many important areas. John Mueller (1989) and James Ray (1989) have discussed changes in norms relating to slavery and to the use of force. Goertz and Diehl (1992) and David Strang (1991) have looked at norms of decolonization. Kegley and Raymond (1990) have looked at norms in regard to alliance behavior. Starr (1991c) has investigated norms in regard to the diffusion of democracy in the international system.

exist in the international arena. This idea is the accepted wisdom that "anarchy" does not necessarily mean "chaos." All these constants, including the Westphalian trade-off, must be seen within the context of any historical period. These contexts will reflect the changing interests of states, which are then reflected in the substance of international law. Such contexts and interests affect the way we answer our central question: how to manage interdependence? By framing the issue in this way, we can better reconcile the differences separating Realist and Liberal theories on this dimension of world politics and perhaps be able to arrive at some form of Realist-Neoliberal complementarity.

Divergencies: Basic Views of International Law

The foregoing characterization of anarchy captures the basic Realist view of international law (as represented by Morgenthau [1973] and Waltz [1959]). From a Realist perspective, an international system is anarchic when there exists no legitimate authority that sits above the states in the system. Part of the Realist view of international relations is that international law is most often not relevant to how states will behave within this anarchic system. International law lacks clear and constant relevance because it lacks the centralized enforcement mechanisms and capability that are seen to represent law. That is, to Realists, international law is of no consequence because it is not really law.

To Realists, given that the anarchic system lacks centralized authority and that states are endowed with the special legal status of sovereignty (which importantly includes a monopoly over the use of force), states must depend, ultimately, upon self-help against other states. Other states cannot be constrained by the threat of centralized enforcement; alliance commitments cannot be enforced as can domestic contractual arrangements. The structure of the anarchic system is thus *permissive:* war, or aggression, or coercion through the threat of force, can occur because there is nothing to stop it (Waltz 1959). Thus, the *opportunity for war* always exists within such a system.[4]

According to the Realist and Neorealist account, given this structure of opportunities, states must (or should) rely on self-help. A key component of Realist thought that too often is overlooked by Neorealists (and most problematically by Structural Realists; see Shimko 1992) must also be included at this point—human nature. A strand of Realism found in writers as diverse as Machiavelli, Hobbes, or Niebuhr focuses on human

---

4. See Most and Starr 1989, chapter 2 for a discussion of the wide range of phenomena—at quite different levels of analysis and explanation—that are "permissive" factors for war. These issues are also explored in depth in Cioffi-Revilla and Starr 1995.

nature as "evil, sinful, power-seeking" (Dougherty and Pfaltzgraff 1981, 85). With a permissive international system and the inherently evil nature of humans, states must be prepared to defend themselves in a Hobbesian environment of the potential war of all against all. To do so, diplomats must be concerned with power in terms of military capability. In Hans Morgenthau's (1973, 27) famous words, "International politics, like all politics, is a struggle for power."

These conditions also drive diplomats to a conservative answer in responding to the question of how much capability is sufficient to deal with worst-case scenarios: how much is enough? Never knowing how much is enough, Realists conclude that states should seek to maximize their military power. The inevitable consequence of each state increasing capabilities to deal with international anarchy is the well-known *security dilemma,* where any one state's security increases the insecurity of the others.[5] The drive for more capability derives in part from the inability to distinguish intentions from capabilities; one must protect against capabilities because intentions are unknown. However, given that humans are evil, it would be best to prepare for the worst. The worst means that other states will be tempted to violate existing rules and will fail to comply with them when compliance compromises national interests. That is, states will choose to defect—to give in to the "rational" temptation to pursue short-term individual interests—rather than cooperate in the Prisoner's Dilemma situations that encourage noncompliance with agreements. Large numbers of such situations have been generated by the meta-Prisoner's Dilemma of the anarchic international structure.

Within such a system, a positivist view that law is made by states and requires the consent of states is not assuring to Realists. While a positivist view of law is consistent with the conditions of sovereignty and the autonomy of states (which are indeed important aspects of Realism), it does nothing to ameliorate the security dilemma or *guarantee* the punishment for noncompliance required to make payoffs for defection so costly as to escape the Prisoner's Dilemma. A positivist view of law stresses self-interest and consent. To a Realist, it means that states do what they want to do.

It also means that law that lacks automatic and centralized coercive enforcement mechanisms cannot merit the name of "law." To Realists, law corresponds to what Louis Goldie (1973) has called the "common model of the legal order." This model is based on simple pictures of criminal law, law that is "command backed up by force" (Fisher 1969). In this model, law consists of commands that prohibit certain kinds of behavior under

---

5. Recall that the worst-case-scenario syndrome was discussed in the introduction as an analytic failure that could be traced to failure to appreciate that *both* opportunity and willingness must exist for behavior to occur.

the threat of coercive force to ensure compliance. Bull (1977) provides two responses to this view of law and its attendant claims that international law is not law: (1) law does not require command and coercive sanctions to be regarded as law, and (2) international law does entail sanctions, albeit informal ones.

In regard to Bull's first argument, Goldie (1973, 129) clarifies why the criminal law model is only one possible model of law. An alternative is the "facilitative" model, whereby law provides a citizen "with the procedures, with the means of doing the sorts of things he wants to do." This model includes much of civil law, for example, the law of wills or the Law of Real Property (as to procedures of transfer, sale, etc.). That is, much of law has nothing to do with command or the coercive use of force.

Similarly, Roger Fisher (1969, 154–55) adds that even some of the most important law does not rest upon coercive command. He notes, "Governments regularly comply with adverse court decisions. This is true not only for constitutional law, administrative law, and tax law, but even for criminal law." He uses the example of the Supreme Court ordering the Truman administration to return the steel mills seized during the Korean war. He notes, "The Supreme Court had no regiments at its command. It had no greater force vis-a-vis the government than does the International Court of Justice . . . Yet the steel mills were returned." Thus, command based on a superior coercive force is not required for law to act as law.

This facilitative view of law is closely related to states' need for order within an anarchic system. Much of international law has been created to facilitate coordination and cooperation among states, to allow them to do the things they feel a need to do. Because nothing is distributed equally in the international system, and because states must exist in a condition of interdependence with one another, they need to exchange goods and services, to communicate, and to coordinate their myriad transactions. For example, the international law on weights and measures, on international civil aviation, and on the immunities and obligations of diplomats all facilitate the interactions of states, permitting them to trade and to engage in the full range of economic, social, and political interchange required by each to satisfy the needs of their populations and the interests of their governments.

While the first model of law based on coercive command represents the general Realist view of "law" and thus the lesser relevance of international law in the anarchic international system, this latter model of law is much more compatible with the Liberal or Grotian view of the international arena. The Grotian view of a society of states recognizes that there is "neither complete conflict of interest between states nor complete identity of interest," that "economic and social intercourse between one country and another" is most typical of overall international activity (Bull 1977, 26–27). Here, then, is one way to characterize two distinct views of the global arena—one that is zero sum against one that is variable sum.

Most of this book has been devoted to the Grotian reality that states *are* linked with one another in an interdependent system and must deal with one another on a continuing basis. This Grotian reality undergirds the claim that sanctions do exist even in the anarchic international arena and that international law can constrain state behavior in part based on such sanctions. It follows Bull's second response to the claim that international law is not law because it lacks centralized enforcement mechanisms. Such a defense of international law also relies on the concept of self-interest on which positivism is based. Echoing some of the arguments made in the previous chapter, note that in the Liberal vision, self-interest is seen within a mixed-motive game where all can win or all can lose. Again, this vision is in contrast to the zero-sum orientation that characterizes the Realist view that what one wins must come at the expense of the others.[6] Liberalism emphasizes that individual self-interest can be calculated only by taking into account the interests and reactions of the other states as well as longer-term interests of the collective. The Grotian view takes as its point of departure *reciprocity,* which serves as the basis for much of international law.

The Reciprocity Mechanism

Why do states obey international law? What mechanisms or processes exist or are used to enforce international law? These questions return us to Bull's second argument—that there are indeed sanctioning mechanisms, albeit informal ones, for international law. While there are no centralized enforcement mechanisms in international law, there are informal mechanisms of reciprocity—tit for tat or other forms of retaliation. States live in the shadow of the future. If each state violated international law whenever it wanted, order would soon yield to chaos; the future would be unpredictable and dangerous. Clearly, when the stakes are high and when states are in extremely conflictual situations, then treaties, agreements, UN resolutions, and all the rest are disregarded. But most of the time such conditions do not prevail. Like Yossarian, why should any single state obey the rules of the game if all the other actors are breaking them? Order seems to

---

6. This discussion could be greatly expanded to include the current debate over relative and absolute gains, which a number of scholars have used to characterize the differences between Realist models focusing on conflict and various Liberal or transnational models that focus on cooperation. Much of this discussion, I think, can be captured in the contrast between zero-sum and variable-sum perspectives.

be one collective good that states do see it in their interest to provide. Chaos—a truly anything-goes system, all the time and on all issues— would be costly for all states.

For example, one traditional area of international law concerns the rules of immunity extended to diplomatic personnel. These rules were established so that diplomats could engage in intergovernmental communication without interference. Without them, the processes of bargaining and negotiation would soon give way either to more violent forms of interaction or to no interaction at all. A good deal of the very strong reaction against the Iranian government's involvement in taking U.S. diplomats hostage in 1979 derived from this fear. If all governments condoned such behavior, based on justifications like the Iranians' grievances against the deposed shah, then international diplomacy would become impossible. It was left to an unusual and obstreperous government leader, Ayatollah Ruhollah Khomeini in Iran, to set the precedent of supporting actions against diplomats. Even during the world wars and at the height of the cold war, governments had still respected the rights of diplomats.

Related to a fear of chaos is the fear of reprisal. By breaking some rule, such as taking hostages or using chemical warfare (as Iraq did against Iran during their 1980–88 war), a state may be inviting a similar reaction from other states. Although there might be some immediate advantage to such an act, it is often outweighed by the costs imposed by other states also ignoring international law. States restrain themselves because they do not want to set a precedent for certain types of behavior.

Thus, to simplify a vast literature, obedience to international law or the self-constraint of states is thus based on the basic principles of *reciprocity and precedent*. Rules and norms constrain states because they are engaged in an indefinitely iterative game with multiple plays in multiple arenas. In discussing international law, we invoke both "specific reciprocity" and "diffuse reciprocity" as described by Keohane (1989, 150). Here, specific reciprocity is described as "an appropriate principle of behavior when norms of obligation are weak—the usual case in world politics . . ." Reciprocity in this case leans more heavily on the fear of sanctions for rule-breaking behavior. International law recognizes both retorsion, "a lawful act which is designed to injure the wrongdoing state," as well as reprisals, "acts which would normally be illegal but which are rendered legal by a prior illegal act committed by the other state" (Akehurst 1987, 6). The term *reprisal* has a specific meaning in international law. It denotes an action, normally illegal but in these circumstances permissible, that is taken in response to another illegal act; for example, if one state breaks a treaty agreement, the other party or parties to that treaty are free to do so also.

The fear of retaliation of some kind additionally includes the fear that states other than those immediately affected will punish a lawbreaker in some way, not necessarily by similar actions. Such retorsion (or reprisal) can take many forms—for example, the Carter administration's decision to boycott the 1980 Moscow Olympics after the Soviet invasion of Afghanistan, or the imposition of trade sanctions on the Soviet Union, South Africa, and Iraq. If international solidarity among a state's adversaries is high, states that fail to apply sanctions against an adversary may themselves be punished (see Axelrod 1986). For example, punitive actions were taken against states, such as Jordan, that appeared to be disregarding the almost total UN-approved trade sanctions applied to Iraq following its invasion of Kuwait. Acting under Axelrod's "shadow of the future," states must be aware that short-term gains from breaking rules that they participated in creating may be offset by future costs imposed by other states.

Drawing on the social exchange literature and general notions of "obligation," Keohane (1989, 150) notes that diffuse reciprocity "is only feasible when some norms of obligation exist . . . These norms may express the actors' conceptions of their self-interest, but their conceptions of self-interest must be broad and their confidence in the good faith of others fairly great." Kegley (1992, 29–30) characterizes reciprocity as a "moral principle of conduct that is universally valid. As a Kelsinian *grundnorm* or peremptory ethic centered in traditional thought about international affairs."[7]

Indeed, there are striking examples of the effects of international law on state behavior, based on the broad principles of diffuse reciprocity that reflect the shared interests of states. One example is the international law on the acquisition of territory. By "intertemporal law," territorial ownership is legal if the means used to acquire territory were legal at the time of acquisition—law cannot be applied retroactively. That is, until recently it was legal to acquire territory through war and force. Even though the UN Charter states that territory cannot now be acquired by conquest, a 1970 UN resolution states that this rule should "not be construed as affecting titles to territory created prior to the Charter regime and valid under international law" (Akehurst 1987, 152–53).

Therefore, Iraq had no legal claim to Kuwaiti territory, and few other states supported such a claim. As Franck (1989) persuasively demon-

---

7. Again, a comprehensive review of the literature on reciprocity would be beyond the scope of this chapter. However, in addition to Keohane 1989 and Kegley 1992, see, for example, Axelrod 1984, Franck 1989, Keohane 1984, and Oye 1986. It is important to note, however, that works such as Keohane or Oye deal with regimes. While in their treatment of regimes they are also setting out the basic logic behind international law, they almost never explicitly refer to international law.

strates, the reaction to Argentina's claim to the Falklands/Malvinas was similar. While many third world states had supported Argentina's anti-colonial rhetoric, only a very few supported its military action to acquire the territory by force. The legal principle of intertemporal law reflects the interests of states—almost every state is composed of territory once claimed by some other state or group. To recognize that as an excuse for military action threatens every state—especially LDCs—as well as international order. While states reacted to Argentina and Iraq through fear of the precedent of using force to retake lands based on historical claims, there was also agreement on broad principles (intertemporal law) that benefited the entire international society.

Thus, as with all legal systems, international law is based on a "golden rule" principle—rule-based behavior to others will beget rule-based behavior, whereas defection or noncompliance will beget noncompliance.[8] The "shadow of the future" is expected to constrain rule violation, or defection, because players can learn from past plays (history) and should be concerned with reciprocity in plays to come (future). And, again, reciprocity is even more important when we recall that there are many games being played at the same time, that states interact in many issue areas that are linked at the same time. The payoff matrix of costs and benefits thus will be affected by calculations of future costs and benefits. This menu will then affect the willingness of policymakers to defect.

As noted earlier, rules or norms may serve as boundaries and trip wires. They alert others to behavior considered unacceptable and permit others in the international society to respond. It is in the self-interest of states not to set a precedent that permits others to engage similarly in behavior considered unacceptable. It is in the self-interest of states not to cross lines that will bring about sanctions from others. Obeying international law is also in the self-interest of states because compliance brings with it a reputation as being a "law-abiding" member of the international society that others can trust and treat as dependable. However, the *informal* nature of this sanctioning system means that there is neither automatic, compulsory, nor uniform enforcement meted out to rule breakers. Thus, with an informal sanctioning system, a state's reputation is of cen-

---

8. The pervasiveness of the "golden rule" is illustrated by this footnote from Kegley (1992, 30):

> Consider Diogenes Laertius' dictum, "We ought to behave to our friends . . . as we wish our friends to behave toward us"; Isocrates' adage, "Do not do to others what angers you if done to you by others"; Pittacus' injunction, "Do not that to thy neighbor that thou wouldst not suffer from him"; Plato's statement of the same principle, "Do to others as I would say they should do to me"; and Hillel's pronouncement, "What is hateful to thyself do not do to another. This is the whole law, the rest is Commentary."

tral importance, inasmuch as a state that regularly flouts international law can expect to fail to benefit from the support of the society of states when it faces another rule breaker. Indeed, that happened to Iran in its decade-long war with Iraq. The lack of support for Iran in its war against Iraq (which was initiated by Iraqi armed forces) and on other issues was due in part to Iran's clear disregard for the norms of international law regarding diplomats, internal interference, and shipping rights, among other offenses; an example of what some observers have called "renegade states."

In a reverse image from the need to coordinate, Liberalism also emphasizes that it is in the self-interest of states to avoid the chaos, uncertainty, unpredictability, and costs generated by a breakdown of order. By recognizing that states have overlapping, complementary, and even congruent interests in getting done the things they need to get done (interests that transcend fears for security in many situations), the Grotian view sees international law as useful, even necessary, as international politics unfolds within a society of states.

The Functions of International Law In the Anarchic Society

On the basis of these broad views of international law, it should be clear that law goes beyond the criminal law model of command based on coercive force. In the absence of a formal coercive enforcement mechanism, international law nonetheless clearly does perform a variety of functions that help states create and maintain order within international society. International law facilitates the achievement of states' needs through its communications and management functions. By clarifying rights, responsibilities, and competencies, these functions demonstrably assist states in the coordination and cooperation required to achieve both self-interests and collective interests within an increasingly interdependent world.

But if the state system is also to be seen as a society, then, like any society, it requires rules or norms to constrain conflict and the use of force and to foster orderly conflict resolution. For example, in his exposition of the Grotian anarchical society, Bull (1977) notes that as with any society, the society of states has attempted to impose restrictions on the use of force—confining war only to sovereign states and then restricting its spread through laws of neutrality and belligerency. International law restricts the reasons or the just cause for the use of war (*ius ad bellum*) as well as placing restrictions on the manner in which a just war could be conducted (*ius in bello*).

Thus, international law serves a variety of *conflict-related* functions:

from the Realist-oriented instrument of direct control (but with only informal sanctioning mechanisms) to limiting the conditions under which a justified conflict can originate, to regulating the legal means of conflict, and to serving a central role in the range of processes involved in conflict prevention, management, and resolution. In this lattermost role, international law can be used to channel conflict through a number of mechanisms and procedures for dealing with conflict.[9] International law can be seen as a method of bargaining, employing processes of claim and counterclaim, whether in informal negotiations or in the formal processes of arbitration and adjudication. In this way international law can substitute for the use of force or violence as a means of contesting outcomes (reflecting Anatol Rapoport's [1960] concept of how to engage in a "game" rather than a "fight").

While the conflict-related functions of international law are self-evidently important to order, one purpose of this chapter is to emphasize the facilitative, management, and coordination functions of international law. William Coplin (1966) has been a major exponent of international law as "a system of quasi-authoritative communications." As he explained, international law serves as an instrument of communication, and, as such, perhaps the primary device for *socializing* policymakers as to the nature of the prevailing consensus in the international system and its changing expectations regarding the rights and duties of international actors.

Hence, the communication function should be seen as a prerequisite for the facilitative function, as the set of expectations to be communicated includes the rules necessary for the simple coordination of behavior required in order to get things done. This process is analogous to the classic "rules of the road," such as the rules specifying the side of the road on which to drive, which color light means stop and which color means go. These rules inform any driver both what should be done and what to expect others will do. In the same manner, international law serves to establish and facilitate routine interactions among states.

Just as important is the way international law can help coordinate the search for solutions to common problems, which is usually referred to as the management function of international law. The needs for coordination and management—given our discussions of interdependence, externalities, and collective goods—reflect *the* key role of international law in world order. As noted, interdependence, externalities, and collective goods can

---

9. For example, Article 33 of the UN Charter sets out a range of conflict resolution processes that states should pursue before submitting a dispute to a UN organ such as the Security Council or the General Assembly: "negotiation, inquiry, mediation, conciliation, arbitration, judicial settlement, resort to regional agencies or arrangements, or other peaceful means of their own choice."

generate highly conflictual situations. In such classic Prisoner's Dilemma situations, sovereign states, looking out for their individual, short-term self-interest will rarely be able to solve such problems and will usually make them worse.

We have noted that in attempting to devise policies that could deal with the dilemmas generated by collective goods, analysts initially developed two broad approaches: (1) some form of enclosure or privatization by which goods are made private and owners given the responsibility for their care, and (2) coercion through some form of centralized authority. However, recent theory and research have demonstrated that such dilemmas can be addressed and solved through regimes—which involve the cooperation and collaboration of individuals or groups, without solutions imposed from some higher authority, and with the relevant participants willing to engage in self-regulation (and enforcement!) in order to achieve some good or to protect an existing common-pool resource.

It is in the theory, practice, and consequences of regimes that international law finds its most important impact on order in the contemporary global system. Questions of regime emergence, maintenance, and effectiveness have all been previously addressed by the scholars of international law. For example, the two primary sources of international law are treaties and custom.[10] These two processes are directly analogous to the discourse on the different ways in which regimes are created—whether regimes are negotiated or are self-generating or spontaneous.[11] In a like manner, in his discussion of the apparent differences between the management of local CPRs and the management of international commons, Snidal (1995) looks at the modalities by which successful CPR management regimes arise—through either evolution or design. Hence, while the analysis of international law deals with similar phenomena and processes, most work on regimes *ignores* this previous thought on international law. And, though not as pronounced, the regime literature also downplays important aspects

---

10. Article 38 of the Statute of the International Court of Justice identifies three major sources of international law: (1) international conventions or treaties, (2) custom, and (3) the general principles of law recognized by civilized nations. Two secondary sources are the judicial decisions of international courts and the writings of "qualified publicists," or legal scholars. The primary source of international law is a formal one, deriving from treaties. But custom, or the evolution of patterns of behavior that states accept and give consent to, is the next most important source. The combination of treaties and custom reinforces the positivist view of international law and shows how states shape international law and how international law can change and evolve.

11. The idea of imposed regimes is not especially relevant to a positivist view of international law. It does resonate, however, in discussions of how third world countries have viewed and dealt with a system of international law created by their former Western colonial masters before they became independent.

of previously developed integration theory. For example, the models of
negotiated, spontaneous, or imposed processes of regime creation are
analogous to the neofunctionalist integration model of Haas, the
Deutschian social communication model, and the federalist model of integration, respectively (see fig. 6.1).

International law is a central component of regimes, one of a number
of regime elements alongside formal and informal rules, both state-based
and those deriving from nonstate actors. The attention paid to regimes
derives from the same concerns noted previously: clarifying what states
have what rights to what behavior, as well as their obligations. Regimes
and international law are used to change the structure of the games in
which states are engaged, by altering the payoffs or by changing the nature
of the choices. Even the informal sanctions of international law, perhaps
as imposed by the IGOs involved in regimes, can alter the costs and
benefits of cooperation or defection.

Arthur Stein (1983) helps us conceptualize the different functions of
international law as well as understand why some regimes are relatively
easy to create and successfully manage, while others are more difficult.
Stein identifies regimes of "common aversion," where the purpose is to
coordinate behavior. They are regimes that deal with the coordination
function of international law, with such "traffic light" issues as having
pilots and air traffic controllers in the international civil aviation regime all
capable of communicating in the same language (English). Coordination is
thus the process of developing policy to avoid some outcome. For example, the rules of the International Civil Aviation Organization are designed
to prevent air accidents. Because of the coordination focus, these regimes
have been relatively easy to form (and often develop along the same lines
as does customary international law).

Stein (1983, 123) differentiates regimes of common aversion from
regimes of "common interest," which require collaboration to deal with
Prisoner's Dilemma situations or ". . . to deal with the collective subopti-
mality that can emerge from individual behavior." *Collaboration* is defined
as agreements designed to avoid the choice of temptation in the Prisoner's
Dilemma and to help the actors choose the second-best strategy, the
rewards from mutual cooperation.

Both types of regimes are contingent on states following their self-
interests while also recognizing that their self-interests are embedded in
broader collective interests. While regimes of common aversion need only
to facilitate coordination, regimes of common interest require management in which states agree to constrain themselves and agree to the ways
in which the collectivity will institutionalize power to monitor behavior,
assess and generate both payoffs and sanctions, and deal with conflict res-

Regime Formation	CPR Management Regimes	International Law	Integration
spontaneous	evolution	custom	Deutschian models
negotiated	design	treaty	Haasian models
imposed		LDC/Communist attacks on Western international law	federalist models

Fig. 6.1.   A typology of analogous processes for the creation of cooperative mechanisms.

olution. These activities can be quite difficult (see for example, histories of the extended Uruguay Round negotiations of GATT or the decade needed to produce the UNCLOS III treaty).

It is important to recall that international law facilitates international communication, including diplomacy. Diplomacy generates treaties, that is, more international law. Both law and diplomacy create IGOs, which, of course facilitate more diplomacy as well as more international law (either formally or through custom). In sum, international law is fundamentally important in the creation, maintenance, and operation of regimes, which generate and promote even more international law.

International Law, Continuity, Change

We return once again to the questions, what is new? what is constant? The anarchic structure of the international system is one constant. A second is the need to reconcile the tension between that structure and state sovereignty with the nature and consequences of interdependence. Realism suggests one view of how to manage the interdependence of the system; Liberalism or Neoliberalism in the guise of Grotian international society suggests another. Realism does not do a very good job of dealing with interdependence in areas where the statecentric system must deal with the nonstate actors of the multicentric system. For example, recent activity in regard to human rights represents an expansion of the domain of international law and a real erosion of state sovereignty. Concepts of universal human rights, embodied in international declarations and treaties, deny states the prerogative to withhold those rights from their *own* citizens. In what is a rather radical departure from the state-centered nature of traditional international law, in the international law of human rights, *individ-*

uals are considered legal entities separate from their state of national origin. Individuals are thus removed from important areas of state control. Human rights norms have increasingly become the basis for intrusion by IGOs and NGOs into the domestic affairs of states. This development strikes at the relationship between the state and its citizens, and thus at fundamental principles of legitimacy and sovereignty—especially the internal supremacy of states and the principle of nonintervention into the domestic affairs of states. Monitoring and publicizing human rights violations by NGOs such as Amnesty International or Human Rights Watch may be the best mechanism for deterring or restraining violators (e.g., see Donnelly 1993).

What Is New? The Conditions of Complex Interdependence

The contemporary answers provided by Neoliberalism also draw from "what is new?" in the international system. We have already provided many of the answers to this question;[12] however, a useful way to summarize what is new is to return to Keohane and Nye's (1989, chap. 2) characterization of "complex interdependence."

The first aspect of complex interdependence draws attention to the multiple linkages that connect states and in so doing takes cognizance of the whole range of transnational relations that bypass the high-level decision makers of governments and the whole range of nonstate actors in the international system. What is new is the increasing consequence of nonstate actor behaviors, a consequence that can be explained by the growth of interdependence and the ability of even the "smallest" or "weakest" actors to have an impact on a system linked by networks of vulnerability. What is new are the technologies of the "microelectronic revolution" that increase the ability of individuals and groups to penetrate the "hard shell" of the sovereign state, create multiple channels of communication, and through new forms of communication and transportation produce ever greater levels of interdependence among all international actors (see also Goodman 1993). What is new is the whole multicentric system composed of "sovereignty-free" actors that interact with states and form an important part of the environment within which states exist.

The second component of complex interdependence follows from the argument that there is no consistent hierarchy of issues—there are multiple issues, they cut across traditional domestic-foreign distinctions, and military security does *not* dominate the hierarchy. In conjunction with the

---

12. For another perspective on "what is new?" see Zacher 1992 and Zacher and Matthew 1995, for arguments that the international system is in "a process of fundamental change."

first aspect of complex interdependence, there is a newly consequential transnational relations that blurs the lines that Realists claim separate domestic and foreign politics. This separation is crucial to challenging a number of the central assumptions or components of Realism. These components include defining the national interest as power, the lack of universal moral principles, or the "autonomy of the political sphere" (Dougherty and Pfaltzgraff 1981, 99–100).

Of more consequence is the increasing importance of economic, ecological, and social issues in all areas of the world, especially since the end of the cold war. Kegley notes that different problems are likely to replace the threat of East-West ideological discord and military aggression (1995, 6). The end of the cold war, rather than meaning the end of history in Fukuyama's (1989) terms, means that different issues will be of importance to different states at different times. Accordingly, what is new is that "how to manage interdependence?" means more than alliances and balance of power being used to deal with security interdependence.

This last statement becomes even more crucial when the final component of complex interdependence is noted: "Military force is not used by governments toward other governments within the region, or on the issues, when complex interdependence prevails" (Keohane and Nye 1989, 25). How will interdependence be managed among states that have given up the option of military force and that are connected by powerful bonds of economic, social, political, and technological interdependence? What is new are the ever growing "zones of peace," the security communities produced by Deutschian integration processes. While the notion of an international "anarchical society" itself is not new—indeed, that is what we have argued here—there are new conditions creating a society with more complex and stringent sets of expectations and norms.

What is more, these expectations and norms are different from those that dominated an international system giving rise to, and fostering, the continued applicability of Realism. What is new is the spread of democracy throughout the globe—which will be addressed as a central component in the next chapter. Democracy, it has been shown, is a key component to successful integration and the creation of security communities (Russett and Starr 1996, chap. 14). Research has demonstrated that pairs of democracies do not go to war against one another. Thus, it is in groups of democracies that form Deutschian security communities that the Realist perspective, and its approach to managing interdependence, is the most irrelevant in terms of conceptualization and explanation.

Bruce Russett (1993a, 1993b) indicates how the newly emergent group of democracies might have a significant impact on the system. When the international system consisted mostly of autocratic or authoritarian states, it would have been very risky for democracies to behave on the basis of democratic norms; norms resembling those advocated by liberal proponents such as Immanuel Kant and Woodrow Wilson. However, Russett (1993a, 281) notes that "A system composed substantially of democratic states might reflect very different behavior than did the previous one composed predominantly of autocracies . . . A system created by autocracies several centuries ago might now be re-created by a critical mass of democratic states."

What Is Constant?

The tension between Realism and Neoliberalism parallels the tension between sovereignty and interdependence that comprises the Westphalian trade-off. The state system structure has always been anarchic, and yet states have always had to manage some degree of interdependence. There has always been a need for order and regulators to help bring it about. The solutions have all rested upon some variety of decentralized, informal sanctioning mechanisms. Realism's version of "how to manage interdependence?" derived from a view of the Westphalian trade-off that stressed autonomy over interdependence and viewed power as control over military capabilities. This perspective culminated in the balance of power as the key mechanism for the maintenance of world order. The balance of power was generally conceived of as a deterrence process that threatened transgressors with unacceptable costs and was based on fluid and flexible alliances as well as domestically created military capability.

Neoliberalism's version of "how to manage interdependence?" is, on the other hand, based on a set of changing conditions, which stresses the interdependence side of the Westphalian trade-off and thereby embraces a very different notion of "power," one elaborated in previous chapters. Its alternative vision is one centered on sensitivity, vulnerability, and bargaining among states that have largely eschewed the use of the military option. As the state system has developed (matured?) and greater ties of interdependence have emerged, informal sanctioning mechanisms, also based on deterrence processes, have developed. International law has depended on self-interest and reciprocity—fear of the costs others could impose on rule breakers.

In the twentieth century, the deterrence processes of the balance of power have evolved under conditions of increased interdependence, the growth of democracy, the emergence and growth of zones of peace, and norms against the use of force. Peacetime alliances have attempted to maintain order through collective defense. In collective defense, the group of allied states let potential adversaries know that an attack on one was an attack on all. The twentieth century has also seen the development of two universal international organizations, the League of Nations and the United Nations, that have applied collective security with growing success and relevance. Collective security also involves letting potential aggressors know that their actions will be responded to by the collectivity. In collective security, this threat applied equally to organization members as well as those outside the organization. The careful observer will note that both collective defense and collective security work on the *same* principles of deterrent sanctions as does the balance of power.

We have a set of elements, then, which may be used to develop some points of complementarity between Realist and Liberal perspectives. Realism and Neoliberalism can be brought together by viewing them as (most often quite) different positions on a continuum rather than exclusively rival approaches. With the same anarchic system structure, the same decentralized sanctioning mechanisms, and the same deterrence process that characterized the balancing mechanisms of Realism, the Neoliberal can point to changing conditions that now provide a setting in which international law, international organizations, and regimes can play a central role as system regulators.

Clearly the Realist perspective was more accurate during certain historical periods and under certain interpretations of the Westphalian trade-off (let me direct the reader to Most and Starr's 1989 discussion of "nice laws"[13]). Yet, as I have sought to demonstrate in this chapter, some of the conditions that affect that trade-off have changed, while others touch on aspects of Realism and Liberalism that require each other's account to provide a fuller explanation of how international law contributes to world order. Therefore, rather than setting Realism and Neoliberalism up as exclusive and contending explanations, rather than asking which perspective or model is "right" or "wrong," this discussion has directed us to follow the advice of Most and Starr (1989, 181) and instead ask, "under what conditions does each model/theory work?"

One such condition—which, since Kant, has been considered as having a major impact on the nature of the system and how states would act in that system—is democracy. How many democracies exist in the global system at any point in time, and what proportion of the system are democracies? How do democracies interact—with one another and with non-democracies? While introduced briefly earlier, the condition of democracy in the system is the focus of chapter 7.

---

13. Most and Starr (1989) discuss "nice laws" in terms of the need to understand that many generalizations are important and useful despite a lack of universality. They argue the need to understand the *contingent* nature of relationships and thus the proper specification of the contingencies or contexts within which relationships could be expected to hold. (See also Boynton 1982.)

CHAPTER 7

Democracy, Peace, and Integration in the Westphalian System

Introduction: The Question of Democracy

The issue of democracy, and why it is important to the current discussion, goes well beyond the basic (but extraordinarily crucial) finding that pairs of democracies rarely, if ever, go to war. In chapter 5 we discussed the anarchic nature of the international system as a constant. But within that constancy, other conditions change. One such change is the rise of an international system that is now filled with democracies. We must then ask: How are states to adapt to a system of democracies? Do the (mostly Realist) assumptions about the environment, incentives, and nature of the anarchic system still apply when the units in that system are democracies rather than various forms of nondemocratic, authoritarian autocracies?

We need to look at the recent (and still growing) literature on democracy and the democratic peace in order to understand *why* a system of democracies should make a difference and thus require adaptation; that is, "what has changed?" Although starting with the question of democracy and war, this question will lead to a discussion of a set of issues raised about the democratic peace in terms of how those issues are reflected in the Deutschian theory of integration. Perhaps the most important of these issues is the idea that states can integrate, interact, and *be at peace*—yet still maintain their "sovereign" independence. That is, this chapter returns to the positive ways in which interdependence can be managed, stressing a major factor or variable that was not stressed earlier—democratic government. If democratic states interact differently, and thus create new patterns of behavior, then the nature of the system to which they as well as other actors must react and adapt has also changed.

Not only does the discussion of democracy challenge Realist views on conflict, cooperation, and the role of norms, it challenges central Realist assumptions about the distinction between domestic and international politics and possibilities for system change without war. Indeed, including the nature of governments and societies and how they can have an impact

111

on state behavior in the international system forces us to face a part of the context or environment generally ignored in Realist analyses—the two-level interaction of domestic and foreign politics.

In one of the "state of the discipline" review essays published by the American Political Science Association, Bruce Russett (1983) "revisited" the debate over the importance and direction of the effects of internal factors versus external factors. Russett saw this debate as one of the major themes in an overview of the international relations and foreign policy literature. Indeed, the search for the discovery of the linkages between internal and external policy, factors, and behavior continues to be a central focus of academic investigation. Siverson and Starr (1992, 1) observed:

> The relationship between internal and external factors in the explanation of international politics and foreign policy may be seen as an academic equivalent to the quest for the Holy Grail—many have searched for it; the search has taken place over long periods of time and in diverse research areas; its location has been the subject of many theories; and its existence has been the source of continual debate. Many signs point to the reality of such internal-external linkages, but a systematic, empirical connection has been hard to demonstrate consistently.

The internal-external linkage question raises yet another challenge to central assumptions of Realism: the separation of internal policy from foreign policy and the claim to the centrality of the impact of the distribution of power within an anarchic system. This latter assumption is of special importance to Structural Realists (and Neorealists). The internal-external challenge becomes even greater when the phenomenon under investigation is the relationship between democracies and peace. A growing body of theoretical and empirical literature has come to focus on the relationship between democratic government and foreign policy behavior, especially the frequency and targets of war. Two questions have dominated this literature. The first asks if democracies are simply more peaceful than nondemocracies. Research in this area, starting with Richardson 1960, Rummel 1968, and Small and Singer 1976, has presented a strong case that democracies are about as war-prone as nondemocratic states.[1]

The second question, which continues to be a major area of scholarly inquiry as well as concern to policymakers, is the hypothesis that democ-

---

1. The first (and continuing) dissent from this finding was by Rummel (1983). Responses to Rummel's early arguments that democracies are more peaceful, by such scholars as Chan (1984), Weede (1984), Garnham (1986), and Maoz and Abdolali (1989), provided evidence against Rummel's conclusion and reinforced a consensus that democracies have

racies do not (or only rarely) go to war against one another. I will refer to this hypothesis here as the *democratic peace proposition* (to be noted as *DPprop*). The empirical findings across a number of studies have produced a consensus in support of this hypothesis. For instance, early studies by Maoz and Russett (1992, 1993; see also Bremer 1992) review a range of factors—alliances, contiguity, wealth, and political stability—in a search for statistical artifacts that would account for lack of war between democracies. None are found. Their strongest results reflect the amity between stable democracies. Finding a consistent pattern between democratic dyads and peace also challenges a system of Realist thought that both argues and assumes that such behavior should not—could not—happen.

Substantively, for both scholars and policymakers, the issues raised in this literature are particularly pertinent in an era of the apparent triumph of Western liberal democracy (Fukuyama 1989) and the spread of democratic forms and processes across the globe (e.g., Starr 1991c, 1995). An interesting theoretical puzzle is how to reconcile the two areas of research consensus. What is there about democracy that permits democratic states to fight nondemocracies with some regularity but that inhibits war between two democracies?

What Is to Be Explained?

As noted, there has been a veritable explosion of work on the democratic peace. It includes empirical analysis of the relations among democracies, theoretical or analytic discussions of *why* the democratic peace has occurred, or critiques of the democratic peace literature. Such critiques have questioned either the existence of the democratic peace, whether or not it truly challenges Realist models of world politics or whether or not it is trivial in terms of prevailing theories of world politics.

However, much of this writing on the democratic peace—whether devoted to analysis, proof, or critique—loses track of exactly what is under discussion or what is to be explained, as well as many of the basic ideas about system and order that have been presented in this book. Many authors simply forget that the democratic peace proposition (or hypothesis, or law, or whatever) is a statement that claims the following: *there is a virtual absence of war among dyads of democratic polities.* Thus, the basic, initial, unadorned democratic peace proposition is about *war*. The basic *DPprop* is meant to explain the lack of war between democracies. It is about a set of conditions that explains the variance in a specific dependent

generally not engaged in less war than countries with other types of governmental systems. However, see Ray (1995, chap. 1) for a review of research that has increasingly supported the "monadic" argument that democracies are indeed more peaceful than nondemocracies.

variable—war. This somewhat tendentious statement of the central concern of the *DPprop* has been made consciously so. The *DPprop* is specifically about the escalation of conflict to the level of large-scale organized violence between state actors.

Given that war has been perhaps the single most central concern to students of international relations across history—and certainly to Realists—uncovering one factor, variable, or set of conditions that is associated with the complete (or almost complete) absence of war is a stunning achievement. The *DPprop* proposes that the existence of a democratic dyad is a *sufficient* condition for peace. The failure to fully or explicitly understand or appreciate this simple observation—by both scholars investigating the *DPprop* and a newfound set of critics—is responsible for much of the lack of clarity in analysis.

The aforementioned observation does not mean that we must look only at war between democracies and then stop. Much of the debate, as will be discussed subsequently, is about the nature and generalizability of the theories developed to explain the *DPprop.* One way to evaluate theories and to compare their relative explanatory power is to see what else they can do for us and how far their logic can take us in understanding other phenomena; here, what other behaviors, outcomes, or events are implied by the theories that explain the *DPprop?* If we have a theory that we think works, then what else should we expect to see? As suggested at the conclusion of chapter 6, it would be more useful not to ask which theory is "correct," or works "best," but to which explanation works best under what conditions. Each theory or model should be looked at as a "story" that not only produces some particular outcome (peace in democratic dyads), but, under certain conditions, other outcomes as well.

Such an approach to theory, of course, follows the Lave and March (1975, 19–20) procedure for the development of disciplined speculation in the social sciences:

1. Observe some facts.
2. Look at the facts as though they were the end result of some unknown process (model). Then speculate about processes that might have produced such a result.
3. Deduce other results (implications-consequences-predictions) from the model.
4. Then ask whether these other implications are true and produce new models if necessary.

Therefore, if some explanation is set forward for the *DPprop,* what else should we expect to follow from that explanation or model? And, does empirical research support such expectations? It is here, regarding Olson's (1982, 13) notion of "consilience," that we can move beyond simply "war."[2]

Indeed, we must recognize that war is different. It is not simply conflict. It is not the same as escalation, minor incidents, intervention, or even covert operations, all of which have been investigated as "tests" of the *DPprop.* While war can be subsumed under more general forms of social conflict, and while war may also be seen as the ultimate stage of a conflict process or of a conflictual escalatory process, war *is simply not the same phenomenon* as either social conflict or escalation. The argument will be presented that for certain analyses of the *DPprop,* democracy must be seen as a "threshold" phenomenon; that certain questions require proof that some state has clearly crossed into a condition that all participants or observers recognize as being "democratic." The same argument must also be made here for war. While the exact levels of casualties, duration, or capabilities committed can be debated, war is more than a militarized incident, a minor incursion, or the like. War involves sustained use of organized military capabilities under the command of governments. War's defining feature is a large-scale, organized violence that either imposes heavy costs on the participants or creates the potential for the participants to suffer heavy costs (see Most and Starr 1989, chap. 4; see also the articles in Bremer and Cusack 1996).

War is considered the ultima ratio by Realists; that is, the ultimate form of self-help to which states may resort in the anarchic Westphalian system. Indeed, throughout much of history of the Westphalian system, one of the defining elements of the sovereign state was its right under international law to wage war. In distinction from the post–World War II legal regime that has made aggressive war illegal (and has placed strong constraints on any use of force beyond that of self-defense), war had simply been a special legal condition that could exist between states. Thus war was, and was perceived as, an integral component of the anarchic Westphalian state system.

Yet, the *DPprop* (whatever the theory one attempts to use to explain it) makes a simple empirical claim—that war does not occur in democratic dyads.[3] To Realist critics, this appears to be a radical claim. If, however, the *DPprop* is placed within the context of the peace created by processes of integration, the position is not so radical. After all, both the theory and the findings reported in the integration literature have presented exactly

2. Olson (1982, 13) notes, "If a theory explains facts of quite diverse kinds it has what William Whewell, a nineteenth-century writer on scientific method, called 'consilience.'" I wish to thank Steve Chan for pointing out Olson's use of this idea.

3. Or, that war has occurred in only a very few, extraordinarily rare, cases.

the same type of challenge to Realism by identifying state behavior that, according to Realists, was not supposed to occur in the international system (or, if it did occur, was to be trivial in nature).[4] It is obvious that integration theories and studies are not being attacked by Realist critics in a manner similar to the current response to the democratic peace literature (see, for example, Spiro 1994; Layne 1994). Integration in world politics cannot be ignored in commentary and critique of the democratic peace. A key theme to be developed in this chapter is that the phenomenon called the *DPprop* is a subset of the processes and results of integration (especially the Deutschian model of integration).

The War-proneness of Democracies: Monadic and Dyadic Versions

Are democracies more peaceful than other states? Though not strongly supported by systematic empirical studies, some Kantian-oriented theories of democratic behavior argue that democracies should be more peaceful, based upon the notion that because citizen consent is required, democratic culture per se creates more peaceful states. In dealing with this question, Maoz and Abdolali conclude (1989, 20):

> The nation-level analyses reveal that, with few exceptions, politically free or politically and economically free polities are neither more conflict prone nor less conflict prone than nonfree polities. This finding is extremely robust. It is sustained over specific attributes of political systems, over aggregated measures of political and economic freedom (. . . regime types), and over virtually all the conflict attributes we examined.

This investigation of the general—monadic—war behavior of democracies is important because it delimits the democracy-war question. The empirical research demonstrates that democracies are not just simply peaceful—or pacifist—states. The characteristics of a single state (whether or not it is a democracy) are not adequate for the explanation of war—which is essentially dyadic behavior with interdependent outcomes. That is one of the central problems discovered in the study of war by Most and Starr (1989, esp. chaps. 3 and 4) through their analyses of research design and the logic of inquiry. The opportunities available to democracies and, more important, their willingness to take advantage of those opportunities appear in general to be no different than the opportunities and willingness that characterize nondemocratic states. For war to occur, at least two

---

4. For this view of Deutschian integration theory, see Puchala 1981 and Lijphart 1981.

states require both opportunity and willingness. For democracies to have a general relationship to war—to be less war-prone—they would need to be unwilling to enter into war regardless of the opportunities available. Such is clearly not the case.

Thus, theoretically, the crucial question must be designed and studied at the *dyadic* level. If there is a crucial relationship between democracy and war, it is limited to democratic-democratic dyads. Returning again to Most and Starr (1989, chap. 5), this conclusion indicates the importance of "nice laws." While a general democracy-war relationship does not hold in terms of the peacefulness of democracies per se, a more limited democracy-democracy relationship apparently does hold. In the nice-law tradition, it means we are looking at a relationship contingent on the governmental makeup of both members of the dyad. This contingent condition, limiting the study to a specific subset of states, also indicates that the theoretical issue goes beyond simply stating that democracies lack the willingness to engage in war.[5]

While they investigate both the monadic and dyadic questions, Maoz and Abdolali (1989, 4) also look at a third: Does the level of conflict in the international system decline as the number of politically free states increases? This question has direct relevance for our concern with order in the international system, as well as the general change in context raised in chapters 5 and 6. As noted in the opening of this chapter, a discussion of the systemic level of democracy and conflict will help indicate why the *DPprop* is important, both theoretically and substantively in our concern with interdependence and order.

Democratic Impact on the International System

In looking at the systemic impacts that democracies may have, Maoz and Abdolali (1989, 27) conclude that the "proportion of democratic-democratic interaction opportunities had a negative effect on the number of wars" over the 1816–1976 period. This conclusion is used to reinforce the findings regarding the question of whether or not democracies are necessarily more peaceful, and of the *DPprop*. The key point is that more

---

5. The "specific subset of states" requires further specification. Until recently, democratic states have come from the wealthier, developed set of Western states. Indeed, references to integration theory and the study of integration processes derive almost totally from the experience of Western Europe. So a caveat is clearly in order regarding the applicability of these phenomena to developing, non-Western states. With that in mind, I have two responses: (1) as a working hypothesis, or as the Lave and March "story" to be used until empirical analysis requires revision and reformulation of our model, I will use these developed, Western models as jumping-off points for analysis; (2) even if only applicable to developed Western states, these new patterns of behavior become part of the systemic environment and thus affect *all* actors; all actors face new contexts to which they must adapt.

democracies produce more possible democratic dyads, which in turn lower the level of war in the system.

This finding increases in substantive importance when added to the conclusion that there has been a worldwide movement toward greater numbers of democracies, with strong indications of the diffusion of democracy in the international system in the 1974–1987 period (e.g., see Starr 1991c). *If* the lack of war between democracies is a true and robust relationship, and *if* there is a continuing trend of democratic diffusion in the system, then the international system as a whole will be more peaceful (see also Russett 1990; 1993b).

Other benefits follow from the existence of a more peaceful system. Much more complex than the simple democracy–economic development theories of the 1950s and early 1960s are contemporary views based on interdependence, integration, and transnational theories linking democracy, economic growth, and peace (see, for example, Russett and Starr 1996, chaps. 8, 14, and 15; Russett 1987; Oneal et al. 1996). Greater numbers of democracies should be of help in generating economic growth and the more equitable distribution of that growth. Peace is both a consequence of this process and a cause of greater growth. Even without a direct dollar-to-dollar "peace dividend," if a world of increasing numbers of democracies lowers the probability and threat of war, the enormous sums spent globally on defense could be substantially reduced.

However, for the conclusion of more democracies generating more democracies and thus systemic peace to hold, we need to understand more fully why democratic dyads are peaceful. Will existing and future democracies and democratic dyads keep to this pattern, or will war among democracies become more frequent or approach the normal frequency of war among other types of dyads? We can only answer these questions if we can set out theories of why democracies do not fight one another and under what conditions such theories would be expected to hold. To do so in regard to the *DPprop,* it is essential to have a full understanding of democracy—its nature, the processes involved, what makes it different from other forms of government and government-societal arrangements—before one could usefully produce a story that fits and that generates additional propositions about what the world is like. Therefore, the key question asked in the following section is not "how to manage interdependence?" but one question that can be *subsumed* under it: why don't democracies fight one another?

Why Don't Democracies Fight One Another?

There are a number of propositions that might account for the rarity with which democracies go to war with one another. Russett (1993b) derives four competing hypotheses from the literature. Democracies are peaceful toward one another because: (1) they share common ties through a network of international institutions; (2) up to World War II, the few democracies rarely shared common borders, which often generated the opportunities for war; (3) in the post–World War II era, democracies faced a common enemy in the Soviet Union and its allies; and (4) the cost-benefit ratio of war for one advanced industrial state against another was not attractive, and most post–World War II democracies were stable, economically advanced states.

In analyzing domestic constraints on war, Bueno de Mesquita and Lalman (1992, chap. 5) identify a number of "democratic puzzles," the first of which is that democracies do not fight one another. They outline three hypotheses (called "hunches") as to why this may be: (1) that democracies are like-minded, sharing similar liberal economic and political policies; (2) that democracies share a political culture based on individual rights and liberties and thus abhor violence to resolve conflict; and (3) that the democratic process makes it relatively easier for domestic oppositions to mobilize against the use of force, constraining leaders and making them more unwilling to use it against others similarly constrained.

Other hypotheses could be (and have been) generated. These two lists, however, capture the most prominent arguments, including the debate between "political culture" and "political structure" as explanations for democratic war behavior (see Morgan and Schwebach 1992 for a summary of these two positions; also Ray 1995). The political structure argument holds that it is not democracy per se that makes such states less likely to war against each other, but that leaders of democracies tend to be more heavily constrained in their policy-making than leaders of other forms of government. These democratic leaders' limitations include the constitutional and institutional constraints on decision making, the availability of information, government popularity and legitimacy, the existence of an effective opposition, the disgrace of capitulation and loss, and the need for foreign victories (see Kilgour 1991). All these constraints are particularly potent in democratic polities, although constraints on policy-making choices that reduce the probability of war, as argued by Morgan and Schwebach (1992) and by Morgan and Campbell (1991), should be operative in both democratic and nondemocratic states.

Political Structure-Constraints Explanations

As will be argued subsequently, we need to unpack the notion of democracy to understand what it is about democratic government that would account for distinctive patterns of democratic behavior. Morgan and colleagues, following Rosenau (1980), have tried to ask "of what is democracy an example?" Or, what more general process is occurring that explains why democracies do not fight one another? They conclude that the issue is political structure, not democracy per se. That is, countries with structural constraints on high-level decision makers would be less likely to go to war, and democracy is a system that produces such a set of constraints. Their research produces empirical findings that support this structure-constraint argument (although not with clear-cut or strong support).

We can, however, take Morgan's discussion and analysis a step further. If such constraints exist, what else would we expect to find? If constraints raise the probability of governments being more peaceful *because* they are more accountable to society (essentially a monadic argument) and can be thrown out by that society (thus societal accountability is seen to "restrain the key decision makers' freedom of choice" [Morgan and Campbell 1991, 190]), what else would we expect to find? Rather than look at possible democracy-democracy wars, what would we expect in regard to war in general? Under what conditions would such societal restrictions be strongest or weakest?

Gaubatz (1991), looking at the occurrence of war in relation to the election cycle, provides some answers to these questions and thus supports the structure-constraint model. Briefly, Gaubatz finds that relatively more wars occur early in the election cycle of democracies and that fewer wars occur late in the cycle. Thus, Gaubatz's findings support one of the additional expectations generated by a structural constraint argument—late in the election cycle, with the next elections coming up, there is relatively more constraint on decision makers who, therefore, show restraint in going to war. Early in the election cycle, with elections furthest away, there is less constraint, less restraint, and thus a higher frequency of war.

If the structure argument is about accountability, again, what else might we expect to find? The experimental work being done by Alex Mintz and associates tests a "political incentive" explanation for the *DPprop* (see, for example, Mintz and Geva 1995; Geva, DeRouen, and Mintz 1993). This work argues that the leaders of democracies do not pursue war against other democracies because they have no political incentive to do so. The results of their experiments indicate that the use of force by one democracy against another is perceived by the public as incompetent leadership—incompetent in part because the use of force or war is not seen as worth the costs or risks, especially in interactions with states where peaceful conflict resolution is expected (see also Fearon 1994).[6]

---

6. An interesting example may be found in Archer 1996, where he discusses the 1905 separation of Norway from Sweden. After the referendum in Norway showing overwhelming support for the Norwegian government, the Swedish Social Democrat leader Branting noted

Structural or accountability arguments have additional consequences. Recall that a number of critiques of the *DPprop* are based on studies that indicate the use by some democracies of covert intelligence or covert intervention operations against other democracies (e.g., Forsythe 1992; Stedman 1993). Based on structure and accountability, the analysis of covert operations, however, is evidence in *support* of the *DPprop,* not a critique.

The fact that covert operations against democracies would be roundly denounced across the political spectrum, would lead democratic leaders to hide such activities. In terms of Putnam's (1988) two-level games, covert action against another democracy would not be included in the domestic (Level II) win-set: such a policy would lose because it would be perceived as illegitimate. Thus, the use of covert activities against other democracies simply confirms the conclusions of Mintz, as well as those of Bueno de Mesquita and Lalman (1992); such activities are covert because they would generate high levels of opposition. Policymakers keep operations low key—at low levels of violence and levels of forces employed—because higher levels (as they escalate toward war) will bring major societal and political opposition. In large part policymakers attempt to keep covert operations secret *because* the public does not support the costs of such inherently antidemocratic activity (see also Russett 1993b, 12–24).[7]

Still, the constraint argument has important gaps that need to be filled. If constraints per se are the explanation, they should apply to all states so constrained. Morgan's research indicates that this explanation does not hold. The constraint model appears to work for major powers but not for minor powers. It also appears to work much better for dyads of constrained democracies than for dyads that contain constrained nondemocracies (see Morgan and Schwebach 1992). So, while constraints are important, they do not give us the whole story. There is still something about being a democracy that affects the war relationship between states.

---

in speeches that any attempt by Sweden to use force in Norway would cause a general strike in Sweden. Indeed, King Oscar told the Swedish parliament, "the Union [between Norway and Sweden] is not anything, if it is to be upheld by force."

7. Despite both normative and structural constraints, and clear evidence that the cost-benefit calculation will usually work against either covert operations or the overt use of force against other democracies, we know that some elected leaders of democracies do attempt such behavior. The question then becomes what *types* of individuals—personalities, decision-making styles, risk orientations—will push the envelope of public acceptance of violent conflict with other democracies? These questions are central to the ongoing project of Charles Kegley and Margaret Hermann (1995; see also Hermann and Kegley 1995).

Culture or Norms Explanations

This broad set of explanations is based, as noted, on a set of shared norms "fostered by a democratic culture" (Morgan and Schwebach 1992). These norms derive from the Kantian notion of a republican civil constitution that indicates that a "political society has solved the problem of combining moral autonomy, individualism and social order" (Doyle 1986, 1157). In this argument the "norms fostered by a democratic culture" (to use Morgan and Schwebach's terms) are the central explanatory factors regarding the creation of a zone of peace among democratic states. An initial premise of Kant's position is that, because democratic states require the consent of their citizens to go to war, war will be less likely as the citizens themselves will have to bear its costs. That is, democracies require the development of norms of orderly and peaceful conflict resolution within society—norms held by both the citizenry and the policymaking elite drawn from that society. These norms are expectations that all citizens hold for themselves and others. Contradicting the Realist separation of domestic and international politics, this argument holds that domestic norms and expectations are then generalized to external relations. Leaders of democratic states bring these norms to their management of conflict with leaders of other democratic states. Thus, pairs of democracies do not go to war.[8]

Morgan and Schwebach (1992) note that this *expectation* of peaceful conflict resolution among the leaders of both of the democracies in a conflict situation leads to peaceful settlement. If this argument were to hold, then what other expectations should be expected to hold in the relationships between democratic states? Several such expectations come to mind. One might expect conflicts to be resolved more quickly. Or, following norms that promote "social order," one might expect that conflicts would be resolved in ways more satisfying to both parties. We should perhaps, then, expect a broader range of conflict resolution procedures. The general expectation is that, in some way, we expect democracies to treat each other "better." How might these expectations be measured and tested to see if they actually hold?

Siverson and Emmons (1991, 304) pose a research question that can be used to operationalize such a set of follow-on expectations: "do democratic regimes have a *bias* toward each other that is greater than chance?" In the period 1945–65, democracies did form alliances with each other at a

---

8. This view of the democratic peace is what Michael McGinnis, in personal communication, has called the "ideology" of democracy: an ideology that serves as one of the interdependent linkages among democracies. If a government were to deny political or civil rights to its citizens, other democracies would be sensitive (and possibly vulnerable) to that behavior; such a government would be threatening the ideology of democracy.

rate greater than that expected by chance. They also did not go to war with each other at the rather substantial rate that can be expected from alliance partners. Thus, some form of a political culture argument appears to be at work here—similarities in values, norms, or worldviews appear to make alliances more likely among democracies than would be expected. At least one form of behavior consistent with the expectations noted before appears to hold.

But, do democracies simply treat democracies differently? Siverson and Miller (1991) investigate the conflict escalation behavior of democracies. Reanalyzing the Maoz and Abdolali data, they show that there *are* conflicts among democracies, and that some of these conflicts have escalated to levels where at least minimal use of force occurs. On the one hand, this finding would indicate that democracies do not necessarily treat each other "better." On the other hand, they note that *none* of the democratic-democratic conflicts escalated to the level of violence required for coding as a war under Correlates of War criteria (large numbers of troops in a battle zone or high levels of casualties).[9]

Siverson and Miller raise two points. The first is that democracies do generate militarized disputes; there is nothing in their political culture that prevents the generation and escalation of conflict.[10] The second point raised by Siverson and Miller is that there may be something special in the bargaining interactions among democracies, based on a political culture argument, that prevents escalation to war. Similarly, Maoz and Russett (1992) report findings indicating that democratic dyads are less likely to escalate either militarized disputes or international crises.[11] The control of escalation in these various situations may be seen as reflecting the domestic norms of conflict resolution. This expectation, derived from the democratic culture or norm model, has been investigated by Dixon (1993, 1994), who studied the use of conflict management techniques and the escalation

---

9. Siverson and Miller (1991, 10–11) observe:

> It is noteworthy, however, that the large majority of the disputes between democracies did escalate to the level of the use of force by one or both states. *But they stopped there.* One possibility this suggests is that the bargaining interactions between democracies are significantly different than those that obtain between other types of state pairings. (emphasis added)

10. This point is also shown by Maoz and Abdolali (1989, 27), who discuss the impact of democracies on systemic conflict: "The results of the systemic analyses suggest that, for the entire 1816–1976 period, the proportion of democratic-democratic dyads in the system had a positive effect on the number of disputes begun per year. . . ."

11. It should be noted, however, that Maoz and Russett (1992) also find that democratic-democratic dyads are associated with *lower* levels of the occurrence of disputes and crises. These results *do* indicate that democracies treat each other "better."

of disputes (see also Raymond 1994). One of the other behaviors expected
to occur if the political culture argument is valid is found—democracies do
tend to employ conflict management techniques in dealing with one
another, including the greater use of international organizations.

The culture or norms explanation, however, requires substantially
further research to assess whether the additional speculations generated by
that model hold. For example, while Siverson and Emmons (1991) and
Maoz and Russett (1992) provide indications that democracies do treat
each other better in regard to alliance ties or the escalation of disputes and
crises, does this finding hold regarding coalition behavior in general, especially in regard to the sharing of benefits and costs?

One illustrative study may be cited. Starr (1972) investigated the war
coalition behavior of states from 1816 to 1967 in regard to the distribution
of payoffs and losses within coalitions at the end of wars. A cursory
reanalysis of that war coalition payoff data shows that democracies in
democracy-dominated coalitions do not appear to engage in more satis-
factory postwar coalition bargaining or conflict resolution in regard to the
distribution of wartime spoils than do nondemocracies in authoritarian-
dominated coalitions.[12]

Many of the discussions of the "limitations" of the *DPprop* investigate such international behavior as interventions, militarized disputes,
escalation, and the like, and conclude that democracies do not treat each
other "better." To be fair, such studies are attempting some form of the
Lave and March process. However, these exercises do not disprove or
weaken the *DPprop*. What they do say is that some specific theory of why
the *DPprop* occurs, when extended at least in part through its own internal
logic, is not adequate by itself to explain the democratic peace or related
behaviors. That is, for a more complete explanation that is also consistent
with extensions, the theory or model must be more clearly or fully

---

12. One interesting observation can be made using an index developed in Starr 1972,
which measured the degree of ideology/community among coalition members. War coalitions composed either entirely of democracies or of a majority of democracies (based on
Doyle's 1986 classification) had lower community/ideology scores—the members shared
fewer such linkages or similarities—than coalitions with no democracies. This finding leads
us back to research that looks simply at the *similarity* among any set of states, and not just
democracies (or the existence of democratic norms). A number of investigators have noted
the high rates of warfare among authoritarian or other categories of nondemocratic states.
Thus, simply being similar is not enough to keep states out of war with one another.

Starr also calculated a score for the degree to which coalition partners fulfilled prewar
and wartime goals and objectives. Comparing these scores for coalition partners in all-demo-
cratic or democracy-dominated coalitions, we again find that democracies do not necessarily
treat each other better. They do not produce a higher level of satisfaction among winning
partners.

specified. It would be valuable in assessing competing explanations to see which explanations of the *DPprop* could be extended to other behavior, to assess comparative power as well as the limits of such explanations. But, if theories or models fail in these other areas, or do not work as expected, it does not necessarily cast doubt on the *DPprop*, only some single, specific model that purports to explain how and why the *DPprop* works.

How might we begin to unravel this set of alternative explanations? There is varying empirical support for a number of the possible explanations for peace in democratic-democratic dyads. Which of these would seem to be the most promising? One way to deal with alternative explanations would be to engage in statistical analysis of the possible alternatives. This strategy is followed by Maoz and Russett (1992) in a series of bivariate analyses designed to discover if the democracy-democracy relationship is possibly an artifact of the effects of wealth, economic growth, contiguity, common alliance bonds, or political stability. Using the militarized international dispute (MID) data, they find that only political stability appears to have a significant relationship to regime type and dispute involvement in the 1946–86 period (see also Bremer 1992).

While this form of analysis helps clarify the relationships among variables and serves as a brush-clearing exercise, it does not directly address the culture-structure dichotomy or help specify the causal processes at work. One way to do that is to attempt to look at these competing explanations in terms of the broader concepts they represent. Can either or both of these explanations help us understand other phenomena, help us go beyond the democracy-democracy no-war behavior? To do so would suggest stronger theory and explanation.

Expected Utility and Integration

One such synthesis might be found in the expected-utility models developed by Bueno de Mesquita and Lalman (1992). In applying the analytics of purposive choice to the study of war, they propose one answer to the question of why democracies don't fight each other. I will outline this answer here. However, in so doing I will show how their results can be extended to integration theory and Deutsch's security community concept.[13] We then can return to what impact democracy and the democratic peace might have on the international environment, systemic regulators, and adaptation.

---

13. By demonstrating the applicability of the Bueno de Mesquita and Lalman formulation to the apparently unrelated explanation of how security communities work, I am also invoking the Lakatosian criteria of broader applicability and excess content to their model, thus indicating why it is preferable to other explanations of democracy and war.

The brief review set out in this chapter indicates that the Bueno de Mesquita and Lalman dove-nondove formulation takes both structure and norms into account. It does so, however, on the basis of an argument that underlies much of the research on democracy and war. From Kant through Rummel through Saddam Hussein, there has been the notion that the people in democracies do not wish to bear the costs of war. Because they ultimately bear these costs, people in democracies will not want to fight. Because they also ultimately determine their leaders, the leaders will be less likely to go to war, under the constraint of the wishes of the populace. We do know, however, that democracies fight their share of wars. Perhaps there needs to be some balance between the costs and benefits entailed in war for this to occur; the costs of war somehow need to be "worth it" to the leaders of democracies. I would think that these are exactly the conditions under which expected-utility models would be useful.

Bueno de Mesquita and Lalman create an extensive form of "international interaction game" by which they analyze how the sequence of actions taken by decision makers may lead to war or peaceful resolution (that is, some form of reciprocated conflict as against negotiations, acquiescence to demands, or capitulation to the threat of force). They assume that such decision makers behave as if they were "instrumentally rational"; that is, a decision maker has a set of preferences that are both transitive and connected (meaning that they can make comparisons among the outcomes and evaluate them).

What is key to us here is that they present the central problem facing decision makers as that of *separation:* how to distinguish what type of opponent one is facing in terms of its preferences and preference ordering. Under what conditions will the opponent prefer the status quo? prefer negotiations over other alternatives? prefer capitulation to war? prefer war it initiates over war initiated by the other party? and the like. They analyze the outcomes that will be produced with states that might be characterized as "doves" (states with preference orderings that make them generally averse to the use of force, depending, of course, on the nature of the opponent they face), as they interact with other doves or nondoves.

They present a proof demonstrating that if both states are doves, and both *know* that the other is a dove, then war outcomes are impossible. As they note at several points, a crucial assumption is that there is *common knowledge* by each side of the other's dovishness. Common knowledge means there is no hidden information. Common knowledge has been defined as any information that each player knows and the fact that each player has such knowledge is known to every other player. This assumption is crucial, because Bueno de Mesquita and Lalman also show that under *imperfect* information there exist conditions whereby doves could fight other doves. Fearon (1994) makes a somewhat similar argument when he asserts that democracies *are* able to signal their intentions—clearly—to one another.

Bueno de Mesquita and Lalman (1992, chap. 5) apply these results to the puzzle of why democracies rarely fight one another. In the real world, they argue, decision makers can never be sure what type of state they are facing. That is, how does one know that the opponent is averse to the use of force? How does one separate doves from nondoves? In the real world, how do both sides attain the common knowledge that can be assumed in the game model? They say that leaders cannot know this—but that there *is* fairly common knowledge whether or not the opponent is a liberal democracy. If some country is a liberal democracy, then decision makers know that the leaders of that state will be more likely to bear heavier costs than the leaders of nondemocracies; that the leaders will be under greater constraints (including the norms of democracy) and more likely to be averse to the use of force. All of this is known because of a central feature of democracy—*transparency*. This concept covers the free movement of information in liberal democracies, the existence of opposition groups, and knowledge of internal politics, institutions, and debates.

> I have summarized their argument as follows:
> —Two states who are doves and know that each of the pair are doves will not go to war;
> —this requires common knowledge, which cannot be assumed in the real world;
> —various aspects of liberal democracies can be seen as making them averse to the use of force, by the higher costs (constraints) imposed on leaders;
> —most often, the indications that a state is a liberal democracy *are* known and can be used as prior information by decision makers in helping them separate opponents into types (doves and nondoves);
> —the higher the belief that a state is dovelike, the lower the probability that a dove will use force against it.

Democracy and Transparency

The transparency of democracy means that outside observers can see into such states, scrutinize the activity that occurs within the society and political system, and recognize that the political behaviors conform to some broadly accepted notion of democracy and are robust enough to cross some threshold in order to be called democracy. Such transparency is inherent in true democracies. Transparency that reveals the democratic nature of a polity is crucial for Bueno de Mesquita and Lalman's use of democracy as an indicator of dovishness. It is also crucial for how we conceptualize democracy, develop our theories of the *DPprop,* and measure democracy. The Bueno de Mesquita and Lalman formulation only works when each party can be *clearly recognized* as a democracy by the other party. The mutual recognition of democracy (which equates to dovishness) is crucial to the use of the international interaction game to explain the *DPprop.* It is also central to how most other theories of the *DPprop* ultimately work.[14]

Transparency means that leaders and populations of other states can see that a country provides for the political and civil liberties that permit the regularized and legal contestation for political power.[15] In democratic dyads, it means both sides can see into each other. On one simple level, transparency makes war between democracies much more difficult than war between a democracy and an authoritarian regime. One mechanism by which the leaders of states create a willingness for societal masses (and elites) to support and prosecute a war is the creation of an enemy image that involves the *dehumanization* of the opponent. A number of studies indicate that this enemy image is used to portray the opponent as evil or nonhuman in some way—and thus that the use of violence against such an enemy is justified and that the costs of war are warranted.[16] Images of the "Hun" on British posters during World War I or the images of the Japan-

---

14. Note that in Russett (1993b), the chapter coauthored with William Antholis investigates the *DPprop* by looking at the city-states of ancient Greece. While some support for the *DPprop* is found, much stronger support is found for the argument that each side must clearly perceive the other as some form of democracy if "democratic peace" is to obtain.

15. Democratic transparency—the openness of its political processes and the vast amount of economic, political, and social information that is public and generally available—is a prerequisite for democracy as conceptualized in terms of the contestation for political leadership, regardless of the specific definition used (e.g., see Dahl 1989, 1971). Such a conceptualization sees democracy as providing an environment within which oppositions can effectively challenge incumbent governmental officeholders for power in a legal, legitimate manner through prescribed procedures. In order to do so, the range of political and civil liberties commonly understood as those embodied in the Bill of Rights must obtain—freedom of speech and the press, freedom of assembly, freedom from a range of techniques of repression available to a government. It is only through transparency that a society knows of abuses of political and civil liberties. It is only through transparency that a government would fear the repercussions of such abuses. Thus, only transparency can provide the safe environment for effective governmental opposition that is at the core of democracy.

16. For instance, Kelman and Hamilton (1989, 163) note that, "When victims are dehumanized . . . the moral restraints against killing or harming them become less effective. Groups of people who are systematically demonized, assigned to inferior or dangerous categories, and identified by derogatory labels are readily excluded from the bonds of human empathy and the protection of moral and legal precepts."

ese in American films during World War II exemplify this phenomenon (e.g., see Dower 1986).

With two democracies, and the amount of information that flows in and out of each, it is almost impossible to create such an image. If both countries are democracies, it is likely that they share a broad range of transactions and that the levels of transactions are high enough that each society knows a great deal about the other; this too is strongly consistent with Deutschian integration theory. Such transparency means that each party has *too much information* about the other to create convincing enemy images, for either elites or masses. It means that one important component often used to mobilize societal support and willingness to bear the costs of war is unavailable to democratic leaders when facing one another.

This discussion of transparency complements the work of Mintz and Geva, for not only does transparency mean that leaders cannot use the evil or nonhuman image of the enemy, but the reason for that unavailability lies in seeing that the opponent respects the political and civil liberties within its domestic political arena—including the free press that provides much of this information. How, then, can leaders of democracies convince *their own* populations that war is a legitimate and successful policy?

Transparency is therefore also crucial to how we measure democracy and how cases are selected for the testing of our theories. It is not surprising that the cases of possible "democratic war" most hotly under debate involve situations where analysts argue at length over whether or not country A or country B was "really" a democracy—using extensive case materials to prove fine points (see Russett 1993b; Ray 1993). My argument is that if analysts, years after the wars in question, still can engage in tedious argumentation, then it is most likely the case that the states involved, at the time of the war, were also unclear whether the opponent was a democracy. Such debate means that at least one party to the war had not clearly moved beyond the threshold for recognizable democracies. And, it is essential to note, any careful examination of the *DPprop* reveals that it *does not* necessarily cover "almost" democracies! This point is important in considering analyses of, or including, new or "fragile" democracies, or countries in the process of democratization.[17]

---

17. Analysts must employ some *threshold point* above which it is clear to outside observers that a country is a democracy. For the analysis of the *DPprop*, then, it is preferable not to use continuous variables. I am not sure what studies using such data can tell us. Results of such analyses can be thrown off substantially by the cases that fall "in the middle," where the indicators of democracy are "fuzzy" and it is unclear whether some case should be included in the set of democracies or not. While such continuous data may be appropriate for a number of questions regarding democracy, they are not appropriate for the general investigation of the *DPprop*. For the logic of the *DPprop* to be valid, each side must understand that the other *is* a democracy. Continuous variables, such as percentage of population eligible to

Doves, Democracy, and Security Communities

The results summarized here are clearly related to the study of Deutschian integration. The International Interaction Game can help us understand *how* Deutsch gets from a social communication process that explains the development of responsiveness (see Russett 1963) and community to the outcome of that process, namely a security community.

The Deutschian model presents a process of integration based on a wide array of intersocietal transactions that are of mutual benefit to the people involved. The process is based on *learning*—learning that such transactions provide benefits, that such benefits outweigh the costs involved, and that there are positive payoffs to continue such interactions and even expand them. As such interactions occur, and expand, the peoples involved become more and more interdependent and thus raise the costs of stopping such interactions. Returning to both the expected-utility model and Mintz's findings, we understand that if leaders are to incur the significant costs of breaking the bonds of interdependence, then they will have to present compelling reasons for the use of force or war. That is extremely difficult.[18]

Also, as interactions occur and increase, peoples develop greater responsiveness to one another, the expectation that wants and needs will be responded to positively. At some point this responsiveness produces the "we-feeling," trust and mutual consideration that Deutsch called "community." Responsiveness and community arise out of a continuing and growing set of social transactions by which people learn they can benefit, and through which they come to respect and trust others and expect such respect and trust in return. This process is what Putnam (1993, 137) has

vote or indexes created out of political rights, civil rights, or measures of human rights, must be partitioned in some way. Increased suffrage, or some betterment in dropping restrictions on political rights, might occur subsequent to a country reaching this threshold, but such changes do not alter the general perception: the country was clearly seen as a democracy before such changes and at that point is treated as a democracy or dove. For example, Switzerland before 1971, when suffrage was extended to women (a change that would weigh heavily in some measures of democracy), was still quite clearly a democracy and considered one by the other states of Europe.

Measures of democracy must be partitioned so that clear and high thresholds of "democraticness" are established. For example, the data set compiled by Freedom House categorizes states as Not Free, Partially Free and Free. Similarly, Gurr has used the three categories of Autocracy, Anocracy, and Democracy created out of several continuous variables in the *Polity* data set. In both of these cases, there is a mixed-polity middle category that divides democracies from nondemocracies.

18. This is the argument implicit in our earlier discussion of regimes as one possible (and incomplete) end product of integration, an end product that produced most of the benefits of a security community without the added costs of amalgamation.

called "dense networks of social exchange." He argues, "Networks of civic engagement are an essential form of social capital: the denser such networks in a community, the more likely that citizens there will be able to cooperate for mutual benefit." In a similar conclusion, Taylor and Singleton (1993) also argue that community can act to reduce uncertainty and thus lower the transaction costs of solving collective action problems.

This is the process of integration at the heart of the social communication model developed by Deutsch. The most tangible outcome of that process is the security community, a group that, because of responsiveness and community, has given up the military option in regard to their mutual interactions, replacing it with "dependable expectations of 'peaceful change'" (Deutsch 1957, 5). Recall that there need not be the creation of a single entity (amalgamation) to have a security community, but that states may form a pluralistic security community as well, retaining their independence. And, as noted, the basic Realist assumptions about power, military capabilities, and security in interstate relations do not hold for states within a pluralistic security community.

The International Interaction Model helps us understand how one gets from the social communication integration process to the security community outcome. Bueno de Mesquita and Lalman argue that the use of regime type—liberal democracy or not—can be used to increase the odds of successfully separating doves from nondoves. In a security community setting, one could argue that there is no risk or gamble on the type of state, that the probabilities are 100 percent that decision makers are dealing with a democratic state that is averse to the use of force. The interdependent bonds of mutually rewarding transactions and the creation of feelings of community raise the costs of using force to a prohibitive level. If simply identifying a state as a democracy significantly raises the odds of correctly identifying a dove, having a state with whom one has developed mutual responsiveness, high degrees of community, and interdependence creates *virtual certainty of its dovelike nature.*

We are now using learning in another sense. Decision makers must learn what behavior is relevant to the separation of types of states. The social integration process provides decision makers with overwhelming information that allows them to have full confidence in how they separate states. Those states with whom they form a security community *are* doves, averse to the use of force. All the members of the security community have learned that. As such, the Bueno de Mesquita and Lalman proof that two doves with common knowledge must negotiate or stay at the status quo applies. Force will not be involved, war will not occur. This *is* the Deutschian definition of the security community.

As with the *DPprop,* the Deutschian definition of integration focuses on peace; but it does more. As noted, a security community involves not only the absence of war, but more important, the *absence of the military option* in the interactions of the states within the security community.[19] From this perspective, it is clear that the Deutschian theory of integration deals with an outcome that is broader than, and overarches, the democratic peace phenomenon. Thus, an investigation of integration may provide some clues in the explanation of the *DPprop*.

When we look closely at the components of the Deutschian social-communication model of the integration process as well as the neofunctional process model of Ernst Haas, we find *all* the primary components of the two central theories used to explain the *DPprop*. The structural constraints model involves the constraints of interdependence, organizations, and formal laws or constitutions; the democratic culture argument involves the presence of community, responsiveness, shared values, and norms. Thus, key components of the two basic explanations of how the *DPprop* works are found in the two basic theories of integration. Additionally, the theories of integration stress the role of learning in the development of norms of cooperation and a sense of community; they stress the need for mutual benefits and the positive impact of interdependence on the management of interdependent relations. Again, these are key components of theories attempting to explain the *DPprop*.

From an integration perspective, what does it mean when one uncovers evidence that democracies might intervene in other democracies or escalate a conflict with another democracy to the point where the military option is raised? From this perspective, all it means is that there has been, to to that point in time, incomplete integration. That is, the democracies involved exist within a not yet fully formed, or imperfectly formed, security community. Here, under certain conditions, the military option may indeed be raised in certain disputes—but still does not escalate to actual war. Does such a situation invalidate theories of integration? Is there not a difference between claiming that integration does not exist or is a failure, and merely indicating that the processes involved have not yet produced the final end product of integration processes, the security community as Deutsch envisioned it?

The behaviors that are claimed to invalidate or disprove the *DPprop* would *not* be used to argue against the reality and explanations of integration—such behaviors may simply indicate that the processes creating integration had not finished. Or, perhaps even more important for our understanding of contemporary world problems, such behaviors may indicate

---

19. For a particularly good description of this phenomenon in action, see Archer's 1994 discussion of the "Nordic Zone of Peace" (a Scandinavian security community).

that there has been some process of *disintegration*. If this is the case, then we should be looking at those conditions that are specified as necessary for integration; investigating theories of integration to see which of the components were not fully present or which conditions not fully met.

Most discussions of the *DPprop* present political culture or political structure as the basic explanation for the behavior of democracies. Many discussions have also concluded either that neither of these two explanations is adequate or that they have to be combined in some way (e.g., Farber and Gowa 1995). If one looks at the *DPprop* through the lenses of integration theory, then these two broad explanations *must* be used in combination. For the fullest conception of the integration process, both Deutschian social communication and Haasian neofunctional models must be considered. In combining these two models, one includes an approach that begins with, and builds upon, the growth of common norms, expectations, and identities with an approach that begins with, and builds upon, the development of institutions that increase interdependence and constrain behavior both through interdependence and formal agreements on common interests, responsibilities, and obligations.[20]

Neither culture nor structure is individually sufficient to explain democracy, or the behavior of democracies, because they interact with one another and each contributes to a larger syndrome that makes up democracy. Each is an important component of the *legitimacy* of the political system—a legitimacy that rests upon the same conditions that undergird Deutschian security communities. Also drawing upon the work of Deutsch, look at Jackman's (1993, 98) definition of legitimacy:

> A regime is thus legitimate to the extent that it can induce a measure of compliance from most people without resort to the use of physical force. The compliance need not be total, but it does need to be extensive.

As with security communities, in a legitimate system there are expectations of compliance and expectations of the nonuse of force. With such legitimacy, democracies can look at other democracies and see systems where norms against the use of force are important and where governments are constrained by the societies they represent (through both norms and institutions).[21]

---

20. Note that we have once again returned to regimes.

21. As Rummel (1995, 24) demonstrates, democratic governments do not practice "democide" on their own people, and "democracy is inversely related to democide." Rummel's final conclusion is that "democracy is a general method of nonviolence" (25).

These conditions obtain because, as in security communities, there is a "compatibility of political values associated with common political institutions . . . and links of social communication that reflect a sense of community and shared identity ('we-feeling') among the members, including mutual sympathy and loyalties" (Kacowicz 1995, 2). The legitimacy of democracies also derives from the expectation of joint economic reward, one of the Deutschian preconditions for integration. The legitimacy of integrated societies also includes the expectation that there will be a certain equity in the distribution of economic benefits and thus the narrowing of gaps between the richest and poorest in society (Deutsch 1977).

The transparency of democracies means that people inside and outside of the society can see how the political and economic systems work, that they can *participate* in those systems, and additionally expect some "fair" mutual participation in the payoffs. Transparency involves, in part, the open movement of large amounts of information. It would be impossible for any form of free-market system to work without very large amounts of information available to all participants, and potential participants, about supply, demand, prices, performance, and so on. Of necessity, the information required by a free market moves unobstructedly in and out of society; it also moves freely within the society across its political and social systems, as well the economic system. The transparency required in a free-market system thus reinforces the transparency inherent in a democratic political system.

This synergy has domestic consequences in that individuals and groups within a society can understand in what ways the economic system distributes its rewards/wealth/payoffs. When an economic (and political) system can provide positive outcomes for most participants—again, a condition of Deutschian integration—this too promotes societal legitimacy and community through the expectation of mutual rewards.

This synergy of political and economic transparency also creates conditions whereby democracies can draw upon "the shadow of the past"—and can tell that other polities are democracies. It permits and encourages transactions across state boundaries, promoting integration processes between democratic states. If we are concerned with Kantian arguments of democratic norms, or the notion of common culture and values—then the values associated with legitimacy and how they affect integration are important (e.g., see also Huntley 1996). If members of one democratic society with effective levels of legitimacy see another society with similar characteristics, then it would make no sense to *fight a war*. War would make no sense (returning to Mintz's arguments), either as a mechanism to settle conflicts or as a mechanism to allocate values authoritatively (politics) or scarce resources (economics).[22]

Conclusion

The theory and substance of integration as well as the democratic peace proposition are significant challenges and contradictions to the Realist perspective of world politics. This chapter has attempted to indicate the linkages between integration and the *DPprop,* as well as how both alter the environments of states. While it might be possible to discuss the growth of democracy itself as a system "regulator," I would think that most analysts would see the "amount" of democracy in the system as only indirectly affecting the regulation of systemic demands and accommodation, and thus stability. The creation of stability occurs especially through shared domestic norms affecting shared international expectations (normative and behavioral, as in the use of IGOs for conflict management).[23]

We should be reminded that the satisfaction or dissatisfaction of governmental elites (in regard both to domestic and external politics) was a major source of *disturbance* in Rosecrance's (1963) model of system change. The democratic peace—which includes both the relations among pairs of countries as well as the groups of states in pluralistic security communities or zones of peace—is the result of integration or legitimacy processes that promote development and the generation of wealth and a basic equity in its distribution (externally and internally). The same integration or legitimacy processes create informal feelings of community and formal institutional settings (as in the evolution from the European Coal and Steel Community to the European Union).

All of these processes and institutions may indeed be seen as system regulators. In addition, we have witnessed the need for integration mechanisms when the mechanisms of authoritarian coercion disappear. As in the former Soviet Union and Yugoslavia, without integration or legitimacy, the removal of coercive restraints will rapidly produce Rosenau's fragmentation (or what Puchala has called "atavistic forces"). The reality of disintegration and the need for alternative regulators when authoritarian

---

22. In a communication with the author, Steve Chan agues that it is only with the "shadow of the past," that is, long and positive experience with each other, "that leaders are willing to accept each other as doves, thereby running the risk of type-1 error, mistaking an aggressive power as a status-quo one."

23. The reader is reminded, however, of the caveat presented in note 5.

coercion is removed make us return to the linkages between the democratic peace and integration.[24] We are also faced with the question of how to manage interdependence in a world of both growing zones of peace and potentially cascading fragmentation.

Delineating such linkages is a useful way to demonstrate that although the *DPprop* presents a strong challenge to Realist (and especially Structural Realist) models of international politics, it is not unique or radical in its challenge. Second, the arguments presented here also allow us to understand that the *DPprop* fits within an integration framework, that it works according to processes already identified by integration theory, and that integration theory would permit us to synthesize rather easily a number of the "contending" explanations of the *DPprop*. Third, regarding the question of how to extend explanations of the *DPprop,* and in which directions analysts should move, the linkages among integration theory, integration processes, and disintegration with the *DPprop* promise to be fertile areas. Russett, in discussions not of "the democratic peace" but of a broader "Kantian peace," has argued that the *DPprop* is only one leg of a triad that includes economic interdependence as well as international law and organization. All three of the Kantian dimensions can be explored under a broader integration perspective.

If we are concerned with how states adapt to a changing environment, it is important to look for what we think of as fundamental changes. While states retain their territoriality as well as important legal advantages derived from sovereignty, and while the system remains formally anarchic, the reality of an increased number of democracies in that system may be such a fundamental alteration. The number of democracies per se is of interest because of such phenomena as the democratic peace. The *DPprop,* as did integration before it, reveals and tries to explain behavior that Realist models do not anticipate nor explain. As noted, the processes behind the *DPprop* derive from domestic factors, again, in ways not seen as important or well understood in Realist models.

This intrusion of domestic factors exactly complements the nature and process of transnational relations, as discussed in chapter 2. In addition, the common thread of security community–based zones of peace reinforces previous discussions of Keohane and Nye's "complex interdependence." Both demonstrate that "power" need not have anything to do with military capabilities, nor does a traditional conception of military security take prominence as an issue area faced by policymakers. Instead,

---

24. Putnam (1993, 139) provides a useful summary in his discussion of national society and integration: "In other words, reciprocity/trust and dependence/exploitation can each hold society together, though at quite different levels of efficiency and institutional performance."

we are confronted with more and more states with "clearly" democratic governments needing to interact, coordinate, and cooperate with one another in dyads and subsets where the military option is "unthinkable." That is, we are back to the basic conundrum raised by some students of international regimes—how to manage interdependence in a system of states where military power is irrelevant, but where the system is still anarchic and states are still sovereign?

Russett (1993, 137–38) may best sum up the ramifications of the democratic peace for global order and Realist interpretations of that order. Expanding on the ideas presented in chapter 6, let me cite his words at length:

> Perhaps major features of the international system can be socially constructed from the bottom up; that is, norms and rules of behavior internationally can become extensions of the norms and rules of domestic political behavior. The modern international system is commonly traced to the Treaty of Westphalia and the principles of sovereignty and noninterference in internal affairs affirmed by it . . . It was also a treaty among princes who ruled as autocrats . . . When most states are ruled autocratically—as in 1648 and throughout virtually all of history since—then playing by the rules of autocracy may be the way for any state, democracy or not, to survive in Hobbesian anarchy . . . A democracy which tried to operate by democratic norms was at a great disadvantage, and might well shift policy unstably in trying to adjust to the risks . . . The emergence of new democracies with the end of the Cold War presents an opening for change in the international system more fundamental even than at the end of other big wars— World Wars I and II and the Napoleonic Wars . . . A system composed substantially of democratic states might reflect very different behavior than did the previous one composed predominantly of autocracies.

CHAPTER 8

Conclusion: A New World Order?

Opportunity and Change in the Study of World Politics

In the previous chapters, we have reviewed several important features of all international systems, how those features interact, and what they mean for various perspectives or theories of international relations. We have used these features and relationships in order to critique extant views—both Realist and non-Realist alike. Employing an agent-structure perspective—specifically that of opportunity and willingness—we have looked at which of these features have changed (and how) and which have remained constant. We have done so in order to see how international actors adapt and how they have attempted to manage interdependence under different conditions. Rather than merely recapitulating the ideas, arguments, or themes developed in the previous chapters, this chapter will look at some further implications of those ideas. We will discuss implications both for the study of contemporary global politics and for understanding the key problems of the global system.

Complementing observations on the study of world politics that I have made elsewhere, this volume has helped point out that the study of world politics ranges far beyond the continuing (yet increasingly stale) debate between Structural Realism and various "Liberal" or pluralist models. A debate that revolves about the centrality of systemic "anarchy" as the primary explanatory factor or cause of systemic politics is fatally flawed. In this book I have attempted to demonstrate that while "environment," which includes a variety of aspects of systemic structure, is important, this importance does not derive from the formally anarchic nature of the system. The study of world politics is far more than the debate between "anarchy" and something else (with what that "something" is, depending on the specific Liberal or pluralist position taken by the non-Realist interlocutor). Using an agent-structure or adaptation approach, I have bypassed the set of so-called debates among Realists, Neorealists, Idealists, Neoidealists, and so on. I have endeavored to avoid much of the narrow framing of these debates (e.g., Realism and Neorealism arguing over absolute vs. relative gains, or Waltz's notion of "reductionism") by placing the analysis of international order within this broader context.

I have argued that there is more change and dynamism in the phenomenon of the "environment" (or "context"; see Goertz 1994) than can possibly be captured by the idea of anarchy. The concept of opportunity rests on a changing set of environmental possibilities—both constraints and enabling conditions. These possibilities change through the dynamic of technology and the infinite inventiveness and creativity of humans. These possibilities change with every new ideological system (religious or political or both). They change with every innovation in how humans organize themselves for economic or political purposes—including administrative and bureaucratic forms, types of government, and the broader issue of the relationship between individuals and governmental authority. They change with every innovation in how economic, social, and political exchange can take place; in forms of finance; in the creation of new types of organization (from the multinational corporation to supranational IGOs).

Opportunity was seen as having two broad aspects. The first was the existence of some possibility somewhere in the international system. The second was the distribution of the resources and capabilities needed for different units in the system to take advantage of those possibilities. Thus, new opportunities or possibilities in the system have both universal and particular effects. A new technology will affect *all* the units—the invention of nuclear weapons means that this possibility for destruction exists in the environment of all global actors. However, not all states (and certainly, as far as we know, none of the other types of actors) are able to exploit the new possibility. Thus, unlike anarchy, which is a static, systemic given— one of the "constants," without variability and thus unable to explain variance in behavior—this view of the global environment is indeed dynamic and variable.

It is important to remember that anarchy is simply a *permissive* characteristic of the system. The lack of an authoritative hierarchy, the absence of legitimate authority above states, permits a range of behavior to occur. It permits the existence of a global meta-Prisoner's Dilemma (in all its various guises, such as the security dilemma or free riding). We have discussed the nature of this dilemma, however, and how it reflects the effects of interdependence and externalities on actors. We have also discussed the multiplicity of ways humans may be, and have been, able to organize to overcome the Prisoner's Dilemma (how to manage this particular consequence of interdependence). Neither the concept nor the phenomenon of anarchy can help explain when groups of humans are able to solve Prisoner's Dilemma situations and when they are not, under what conditions the

Prisoner's Dilemma is most tractable, what forms or human organization are most or least able to deal with collective action problems, and so forth.

A simple reality faces any analyst of the world politics—that the Westphalian anarchic system, in which sovereign states have interacted, has existed for at least 350 years. The "anarchy" condition has remained unchanged, yet there have been periods of varying conflict and cooperation; individual states have had long periods of aggression and conflict followed by pacific relations; different economic forms have thrived and declined; there have been periods of rapid economic growth and periods of disastrous decline; the system has had no democracies and now an approximate majority of democracies. That is, while the nature of the anarchic system has remained constant, just about everything else has changed. Without belaboring the epistemologically and methodologically obvious: it is impossible to explain variance with a constant.

Opportunity is one useful way to indicate how the environment of international actors can change, and has changed. The ecological triad of the Sprouts reminds us that we must look at both entity and environment and how they interact with each other. It tells us that the environment must be *perceived* by human policymakers (agents), who then react to the images they hold of that environment. The environment of opportunities (consisting of all the various layers within which policymakers are nested) provides an incentive structure that will affect the willingness of policymakers to choose among the assorted options available to them. Both entity and environment must be considered; both opportunity and willingness must be considered. The Realist (and particularly Structural Realist) fixation on anarchy assumes certain static preferences and uniform perceptions across actors. The structures of opportunity discussed here note possibilities, probabilities, and the variability of how they are perceived by different international actors (a metaversion of "where you stand depends on where you sit").

To repeat: both opportunity and willingness must be considered. Considered in regard to what? Considered in regard to how entities adapt to their changing environments in their attempts to cope (that is, to survive) and to prosper (that is, to get what they want in order to develop, grow, become wealthier, more powerful, more secure). What strategies must states follow to cope individually or collectively, in environments shaped by their interdependence? In the preceding chapters, we noted how the newly formed states attempted to cope with the newly created condition of nonhierarchical sovereignty. All attempts to cope were continually confronted with ever changing environmental conditions (including new geographic and geopolitical realities, new technologies, new ideologies, etc.). All attempts to cope had to consider and accommodate the interdependence that has always existed in the state system. Substitutability, as discussed by Cioffi-Revilla and Starr (1995), is thus important—because different actors, facing different conditions, utilized different but substitutable methods of coping.

One reason for the dynamism of world politics since 1648 has been the interdependent system within which states (and an ever growing cast of other actors) have had to exist—an interdependence that made these actors sensitive and vulnerable to one another. Because of sensitivity and vulnerability, even those new elements of environmental opportunity that might appear to be minor—such as the conditions of integration, democracy, the emergence of norms—and would certainly appear to be minor to traditional Realist analysts, had an impact on the opportunity and willingness of states. And, thus, on the requirement that states adapt.

It follows that while the anarchic structure of the Westphalian system has been static, "order" within that system has not. If order is about security against violence, assurance that agreements will be kept, and stability of possession or ownership (from Bull 1977, as noted in chapter 6), then any number of conditions could arise to challenge that order. These conditions include the breakdown of norms that would cause Bull's international society to disintegrate. They include technological innovations, and the (sometimes) related differential growth of military capabilities and economic wealth among states. They include new types of governments and distributions of countries with different governments or ideologies. They include new forms of international organizations. However, in Eurocentric-Realist thought (or traditional geopolitical approaches), the only critical or important challenge to such order would be the rise of a state or coalition powerful enough to dominate the system militarily and subordinate all other states before it. Thus, the primary mechanism—and for such thinkers, in actuality the only mechanism—that could possibly cope with the challenge to order was the deterrent threat of the balance of power.

I have argued here that conceptions of global politics must go beyond those reflecting Realism (and its variants). Order can be threatened in various ways. In the contemporary system, for example, the analyst must address a set of disintegrative "isms," such as separatism, nationalism, fundamentalism. These atavistic forces all threaten order in different ways for different subsets of states.[1] Thus, there are varying levels and types of order for different actors under different conditions. If so, then there exist a variety of mechanisms by which states may adapt to challenges to order. This theme is captured by the numerous references to system regulators in this book, regulators created by states to deal with systemic disturbances and to manage interdependence.

---

1. Donald Puchala raised this point to me in personal communication.

We highlighted the idea of "expectations" in various discussions of international law and regimes. *Mutual* expectations of "normal" behavior, of behavior that is rule bound and that can be broadly characterized by the Golden Rule, are a necessary component of "order." The actors in a system must share expectations (perceptions) that there will not be random violence, that there is some safety in possession, and that treaties will be honored. Any order within a "society," as demonstrated by Bull, must exhibit these shared norms of behavior. They are fragile and reversible, but when such norms exist, they take on characteristics of a collective good. If there is a general expectation of certain kinds of behavior, especially cooperation rather than defection, then the "order" created can be jointly supplied to all actors once created for some. It is fragile in that even a small number of defections (or a set of minor defections) might be enough to threaten such an order.[2]

Order as jointly supplied (and even with some degree of nonexcludability) may be particularly relevant to the post–cold war and post–Gulf War world. The international system was changed by the end of the cold war as thoroughly as those systems that existed before and after the great general wars of the past two centuries—the Napoleonic wars, World Wars I and II. It is instructive that such enormous structural and normative change could occur without some great system-change war as proposed by long-cycle and power-transition theorists. As Mueller (1995, 33) notes, "the quiet cataclysm suggests that, in fact, no war or important war threat is required at all: the system can be transformed by a mere change of ideas."

It is also instructive that the changes in regulatory mechanisms that have accompanied the conclusion of these great wars appear to be missing in the post–cold war era. As noted by Kegley and Raymond (1990; see also 1994), great power conflicts tend to generate bursts in the creation of cooperative norms and institutions; in treaties and in new IGOs. That is, after periods of relatively greater levels of instability, the leaders of states pay greater attention to the development of rules to regulate the use of force. This finding is consistent with Bull's conception of an international society and the need for *any* society to develop norms, rules, and mechanisms to manage conflict.

The great wars led to major peace conferences at Vienna, Versailles, and, analogously, San Francisco. From them came the Concert of Europe, the League of Nations, and the United Nations. These periods of hot

---

2. Indeed, the central argument of Andrew Schmookler's "parable of the tribes" (1984) can be expressed in just these terms—that once one actor defects in regard to the accumulation of power, all others must for simple self-defense. Schmookler's book is, in actuality, about the security dilemma.

war—general in participation, massive in destruction, and of long dura-tion—set in motion inventive thinking about what the world was to look like when the war was over. The natural forum of a postwar peace confer-ence provided the setting for the creation (or reinvigoration) of regulatory mechanisms that might be robust enough to deal with the sorts of distur-bances that were seen as leading to the war just ended. Great general wars change systems. Conditions are changed—actors disappear and new actors appear; the geopolitical landscape is rearranged; new technologies have been tested and disseminated. Changing conditions call for a serious review and revision of regulatory mechanisms.

However, most wars provide not only time, but also *warning signals* indicating that the war will soon be coming to an end. Such signals indicate that the moment for dealing with the changed system is at hand. The end of the cold war had few such warnings. In essence, policymakers and ana-lysts were caught short. There was no broad-based postwar peace confer-ence. We have not yet been clever enough consciously and explicitly to develop mechanisms to deal with the issues of order and the changing con-ditions of interdependence that followed the conclusion of the cold war. We have entered an uncertain period, not simply because the cold war is over, but because the system and its regulatory needs have changed. We need to adapt, but we are having to do so without the prodding warnings of a general system-change war and without the general peace settlement where such regulatory mechanisms historically have been created.

A "New" World Order (?)

It is within these contexts that we should try to make sense of the vast, and growing, commentary on a "new world order." Putting aside the question of how much he really understood the message he was espousing, George Bush's post–Gulf War call for a "new world order" can be interpreted as advocating the renewed use of collective security as the primary systemic regulatory mechanism. With the end of the cold war, and the demonstra-tion that the great powers could cooperate in regional conflicts large and small (as in Cambodia or Somalia as well as the Gulf War), Bush was ask-ing the international community to return to the original vision of a United Nations, led by "five policemen," managing systemic conflict through collective security mechanisms.

During the cold war, the balance-of-terror threat of mutual destruc-tion was the primary systemic regulator. I think that this cold war version of the balance of power had served as a much more broad-based system regulator than many observers realized. Not only did it constrain the two superpowers, but their allies as well. Because nuclear capabilities were essentially bipolar, it meant that the adversarial competition between the United States and the Soviet Union was global. Through sensitivity and vulnerability, all other international actors were caught up in this global face-off. However, it also meant that any other state (or actor) in the system could exploit the bipolar confrontation. The bipolar balance of terror—including the fear that any conflict could escalate to the point of nuclear exchange between the superpowers—constrained not only the United States, the Soviet Union, and their respective allies, but also most other states whose local or internal conflicts could become part of the global superpower face-off.

In addition, as noted by many observers of the UN and the success of IGO conflict management activities (e.g., E. Haas 1986), the cold war severely limited the utility of UN peacekeeping activities. IGO-based mechanisms were of little use in cold war–related conflicts. Only after superpower agreement could IGOs become involved. Thus, cold war balancing regulators not only served as central regulatory mechanisms, the cold war blocked the application of other regulators in any situation of import to the superpowers.[3]

With the end of the cold war and increasing demonstrations that the two former superpower antagonists could work together—as well as with the cooperation of China, Japan, Germany, and the other European powers—it made sense to fumble toward a UN-based collective security. The peace-enforcement activities of the UN coalition during the Gulf War, as Russett and Sutterlin (1991) point out, were as ad hoc as those during the Korean War (the only other example of UN-based compellent peace enforcement). While the UN Charter contains a set of articles that formalize UN collective security operations, they have been ignored. Yet, as Russett and Sutterlin (1991, 72) note, "The Gulf War has served, however, to heighten interest in effective deterrence using multilateral means not under the domination of one or several U.N. members." By 1995, Michael Barnett (1995, 37) could take this "interest" further:

The beginning of superpower cooperation and the experience of the Gulf War stirred a discussion of the meaning and merits of collective security, and the drift of peacekeeping into peace enforcement created a gray zone called "Chapter VI-1/2" operations. Such developments reflect an underlying sentiment that as a security organization the United Nations should possess robust enforcement mechanisms. Sim-

3. So, with the end of the cold war *and* the growth in the number of democracies in the system, IGOs appear to be emerging as much more significant system regulators. The many examples presented in Rosenau 1990 support this proposition.

ply put, it is not enough to be a forum for considering threats to international peace and security; the United Nations must possess the mechanisms to combat them as well.

As with IGOs in more narrowly functional regimes, the UN must also play "an important role in articulating norms of state behavior" (Barnett 1995, 45). The study of international law reveals the rather substantial growth of norms against the use of force, the threat of the use of force, and the restriction of force to an ever more narrowly defined notion of self-defense (see also Mueller 1989; Kegley and Raymond 1990).[4] The UN has been an important participant in the evolution of these norms. Therefore, the UN is also an obvious mechanism for the development and implementation of a collective security regulatory mechanism. States have become enmeshed in sets of regimes that generate order in specific functional and geographic areas. As part of the shift in the Westphalian trade-off toward the management of interdependence, they have developed norms of coordination and cooperation and have relied on decentralized sanctioning mechanisms. Russett and Sutterlin (1991) describe, in part, a movement toward a more formalized yet still decentralized collective security regulatory mechanism situated within the UN.

While regimes in other functional areas provide cues and clues as to how to develop a collective security regulatory mechanism, they also provide us an explanation for the difficulties that face its creation and the critiques of such a mechanism. We have seen that "governance" by regimes is messy—especially in an era of security communities resulting from processes of integration. It is messy because states that do not consider the military option have to work out complex solutions to complex collective action problems under conditions of growing interdependences. For some, particularly those with Realist sympathies, doing so is far too messy when applied to regulatory mechanisms for dealing with security issues. Realists are unconvinced and worried—such regulatory mechanisms lack the clarity and simplicity of the cold war balance of terror.

The reader is instructed to return to the introduction—and the work of Mueller (1994, 1995) or Singer and Wildavsky (1993)—for a discussion of the trend among some current analysts to find ever growing crisis/disorder/instability in the present system. Mueller (1994, 358–59) usefully contrasts perceptions of the current "messiness" with the cold war:

---

4. The growth of norms against the use of force is both a consequence of the growing number of democracies in the system and a condition for that growth—yet another of our complex feedback loops.

Indeed, if the post–Cold War world resembles a jungle filled with poisonous snakes, the Cold War was a jungle filled with at least two dragons *and* poisonous snakes, some of whom were variously, changeably, and often quite ambiguously in devious complicity with one or the other of the dragons. It seems obvious which jungle is preferable—and less complicated.

As noted at the beginning of this book, claims that the post–cold war system is more dangerous and unstable are exaggerated. They do, however, reflect a lack of understanding about systemic disturbances and the appropriate regulators to deal with them. The cold war regulators did moderately well with many (clearly not all) of the disturbances characteristic of the system. With the end of the cold war, *other* (some new and different) disturbances have been able to come to the fore. Many observers have ignored the regulators (centered on international law and regimes) that have been developed over the years to take care of these disturbances and that now must also be moved to the forefront of policymakers' menus.

We must also understand that collective security now appears to be a relevant, plausible, and useful regulator for conflict within a system that still continues to be anarchic and populated by sovereign states and yet is characterized by high levels of interdependence and growing zones of peace. Singer and Wildavsky (1993) depict zones of "peace, wealth, and democracy," distinct from zones of "turmoil, war, and development." They are impressed with the fact that the zones of peace and democracy are growing and that the major democracies ("if not 'the good guys,' at least 'the less-worse guys'") now have "a near monopoly on the most effective military force" (xiv). One way to summarize is to present Singer and Wildavsky's (189) overview of many of the changed conditions we have discussed:

> Seeing tragedy in so many places in the zones of turmoil it is easy to think that the whole world is a mess. But that conclusion misses the profound good news that for the first time in history a major part of the world, which contains nearly all the great powers, faces no danger of military conquest or destruction. The zones of peace and democracy are something new in the world: great powers that do not have to organize into competing political-military power blocs to protect themselves and whose relationship with each other does not depend on their relative military strength.

The newly found dominance of democratic zones of peace present international actors with different challenges, disturbances, and problems than in past systems (as Russett noted to close chapter 7). While new, complex, and challenging to the states that must adapt, there is good news. Based on Grotian norms of society and democratic zones of peace, the nature of this environment is one *in which cooperative management can take place,* in which regimes can work, in which the expectations of coordination and cooperation through rules can have great effect, and in which an IGO-based collective security does indeed have the capacity to work successfully.[5]

Allusion to a "new world order" deserves careful attention, not derision. It is incorrect to point to a newly dangerous or incomprehensible world, only a more complex one where the previous regulator has disappeared and where conditions call for mechanisms of regulation that have slowly been developing throughout the global system. While we may be somewhat tardy in recognizing the change in systems and the ramifications of change, we do have the wherewithal to deal with that change—the concepts, the theories (especially deriving from the study of integration), and the practices of international actors. We must understand what is new and what is constant if we are to manage interdependence into the twenty-first century.

---

5. With the growth of democracy and Russett's "bottom up" construction of international norms and behavior, as well as the processes of integration found in a growing security community of states, the global system can be seen as a working example of Axelrod's (1984) evolution of cooperation.

References

Akehurst, Michael. 1987. *A Modern Introduction to International Law*. 6th ed. London: Allen and Unwin.

Archer, Clive. 1994. *Organizing Europe: The Institutions of Integration*. London: Arnold.

———. 1996. "The Nordic Area as a Zone of Peace." Centre for Defence Studies, University of Aberdeen, Scotland.

Axelrod, Robert. 1984. *The Evolution of Cooperation*. New York: Basic Books.

———. 1986. "An Evolutionary Approach to Norms." *American Political Science Review* 80:1095–1111.

Axelrod, Robert, and Robert O. Keohane. 1986. "Achieving Cooperation under Anarchy: Strategies and Limitations." In Kenneth A. Oye, ed., *Cooperation under Anarchy*. Princeton, NJ: Princeton University Press.

Baldwin, David A. 1985. *Economic Statecraft*. Princeton, NJ: Princeton University Press.

———. 1989. *Paradoxes of Power*. Oxford: Basil Blackwell.

Barkun, Michael. 1968. *Law without Sanctions*. New Haven, CT: Yale University Press.

Barnet, Richard, and John Cavanaugh. 1994. *Global Dreams: Imperial Corporations and the New World Order*. New York: Simon and Schuster.

Barnet, Richard, and Ronald E. Muller. 1974. *Global Reach*. New York: Simon and Schuster.

Barnett, Michael N. 1995. "The United Nations and Global Security: The Norm is Mightier than the Sword." *Ethics & International Affairs* 9:37–54.

Bergsten, C. Fred, Robert O. Keohane, and Joseph S. Nye. 1975. "International Economics and International Politics: A Framework for Analysis." *International Organization* 29:3–36.

Boulding, Kenneth E. 1978. *Stable Peace*. Austin: University of Texas Press.

Boynton, G. Robert. 1982. "On Getting from Here to There: Reflections on Two Paragraphs and Other Things." In Elinor Ostrom, ed., *Strategies of Political Inquiry*. Beverly Hills: Sage.

Bremer, Stuart A. 1992. "Dangerous Dyads: Conditions Affecting the Likelihood of Interstate War, 1816–1965." *Journal of Conflict Resolution* 36:309–41.

Bremer, Stuart A., and Thomas R. Cusack, eds. 1996. *The Process of War: Advancing the Scientific Study of War*. Philadelphia: Gordon and Breach.

Bromley, Daniel W. 1991. *Environment and Economy: Property Rights and Public Policy*. Cambridge: Blackwell.

Bueno de Mesquita, Bruce, and David Lalman. 1992. *War and Reason.* New Haven, CT: Yale University Press.

Bull, Hedley. 1977. *The Anarchical Society.* London: Macmillan.

Bull, Hedley, and Adam Watson, eds. 1984. *The Expansion of International Society.* Oxford: Clarendon.

Caporaso, James A. 1993. "Global Political Economy." In Ada W. Finifter, ed., *Political Science: The State of the Discipline.* Washington, DC: American Political Science Association.

Caporaso, James A., and John Keller. 1993. "The European Community and Regional Integration Theory." Paper presented at the Third Biennial Conference of the European Community Studies Association, May 27–29, Washington, DC.

Caporaso, James A., and David P. Levine. 1992. *Theories of Political Economy.* Cambridge: Cambridge University Press.

Chan, Steve. 1984. "Mirror, Mirror on the Wall . . . Are the Free Countries More Pacific?" *Journal of Conflict Resolution* 28:617–48.

———. 1993. *East Asian Dynamism: Growth, Order, and Security in the Pacific Region.* 2d ed. Boulder, CO: Westview.

Cioffi-Revilla, Claudio, and Harvey Starr. 1995. "Opportunity, Willingness and Political Uncertainty: Theoretical Foundations of Politics." *Journal of Theoretical Politics* 7:447–76.

Coate, Roger A., ed. 1994. *U.S. Policy and the Future of the United Nations.* New York: Twentieth Century Fund Press.

Coplin, William D. 1966. *The Functions of International Law.* Chicago: Rand McNally.

Dahl, Robert A. 1971. *Polyarchy.* New Haven, CT: Yale University Press.

———. 1989. *Democracy and Its Critics.* New Haven, CT: Yale University Press.

Deutsch, Karl W. 1977. "National Integration: Some Concepts and Research Approaches." *Jerusalem Journal of International Relations* 2:1–29

Deutsch, Karl W., et al. 1957. *Political Community and the North Atlantic Area.* Princeton, NJ: Princeton University Press.

Dixon, William J. 1993. "Democracy and the Management of International Conflict." *Journal of Conflict Resolution* 37:42–68.

———. 1994. "Democracy and the Peaceful Settlement of International Conflict." *American Political Science Review* 88:14–32.

Donnelly, Jack. 1993. *International Human Rights.* Boulder, CO: Westview.

Dougherty, James E., and Robert L. Pfaltzgraff. 1981. *Contending Theories of International Relations.* 2d ed. New York: Harper and Row.

Dower, John W. 1986. *War without Mercy: Race and Power in the Pacific War.* New York: Pantheon.

Doyle, Michael W. 1986. "Liberalism and World Politics." *American Political Science Review* 80:1151–69.

Farber, Henry S., and Joanne Gowa. 1995. "Polities and Peace." *International Security* 20:123–46.

Fearon, James D. 1994. "Domestic Political Audiences and the Escalation of International Disputes." *American Political Science Review* 88:577–92.

Fife, Daniel. 1977. "Killing the Goose." In Garrett Hardin and John Baden, eds., *Managing the Commons.* San Francisco: W. H. Freeman.

Fisher, Roger. 1969. *International Conflict for Beginners.* New York: Harper and Row.

Fisher, Roger, and William Ury. 1981. *Getting to Yes.* New York: Penguin Books.

Forsythe, David P. 1992. "Democracy, War, and Covert Action." *Journal of Peace Research* 29:385–95.

Franck, Thomas M. 1989. "The Strategic Role of Legal Principles." In Bruce Russett, Harvey Starr, and Richard Stoll, eds., *Choices in World Politics: Sovereignty and Interdependence.* New York: W. H. Freeman.

Friedman, Gil, and Harvey Starr. Forthcoming. *Agency, Structure and International Politics.* London: Routledge.

Frohlich, Norman, Joe Oppenheimer, and Oran Young. 1971. *Political Leadership and Collective Goods.* Princeton, NJ: Princeton University Press, 1971.

Fukuyama, Francis. 1989. "The End of History?" *National Interest* 16 (summer): 3–18.

Garnham, David. 1986. "War-Proneness, War-Weariness, and Regime Type, 1816–1980." *Journal of Peace Research* 23:279–89.

Gaubatz, Kurt T. 1991. "Election Cycles and War." *Journal of Conflict Resolution* 35:212–44.

Geva, Nehemia, Karl DeRouen, and Alex Mintz. 1993. "The Political Incentive Explanation of 'Democratic Peace': Evidence from Experimental Research." *International Interactions* 18:215–29.

Gilpin, Robert. 1987. *The Political Economy of International Relations.* Princeton, NJ: Princeton University Press.

Goertz, Gary. 1994. *Contexts of International Politics.* Cambridge: Cambridge University Press.

Goertz, Gary, and Paul F. Diehl. 1992. "Toward a Theory of International Norms." *Journal of Conflict Resolution* 36:634–64.

Goldie, Louis F. E. 1973. "International Law and the World Community." In F. H. Hartman, ed., *World in Crisis,* 4th ed. New York: Macmillan.

Goodman, Allan E. 1993. *A Brief History of the Future.* Boulder, CO: Westview.

Haas, Ernst B. 1986. *Why We Still Need the United Nations: The Collective Management of International Conflict, 1945–1984.* Policy Papers in International Affairs, no.26. Berkeley, CA: Institute of International Studies.

Haas, Peter. 1992. "Introduction: Epistemic Communities and International Policy Coordination." *International Organization* 46:1–36.

Hall, Charles. 1996. "Common-Pool Resource Institutions for Ocean Governance." Ph.D. diss., University of South Carolina.

Hardin, Garrett. 1977a. "The Tragedy of the Commons." In Garrett Hardin and John Baden, eds., *Managing the Commons.* San Francisco: W. H. Freeman.

———. 1977b. "An Operational Analysis of 'Responsibility.'" In Garrett Hardin and John Baden, eds., *Managing the Commons.* San Francisco: W. H. Freeman.

Hart, Jeffrey. 1976. "Three Approaches to the Measurement of Power in International Relations." *International Organization* 30:289–305.

Heller, Joseph. 1961. *Catch–22*. New York: Dell.

Hermann, Margaret G., and Charles W. Kegley Jr. 1995. "Rethinking Democracy and International Peace: Perspectives from Political Psychology." *International Studies Quarterly* 39:511–33.

Herz, John. 1957. "The Rise and Demise of the Territorial State." *World Politics* 9:473–93.

———. 1968. "The Territorial State Revisited—Reflections on the Future of the Nation–State." *Polity* 1:11–34.

Hoffmann, Stanley. 1972. "The Functions of International Law." In Romano Romani, ed., *The International Political System*. New York: John Wiley & Sons.

Hollis, Martin, and Steve Smith. 1990. *Explaining and Understanding International Relations*. Oxford: Clarendon Press.

Holsti, K. J. 1992. "Governance without Government: Polyarchy in Nineteenth-Century European International Politics." In James N. Rosenau and Ernst-Otto Czempiel, eds., *Governance without Government: Order and Change in World Politics*. Cambridge: Cambridge University Press.

Huntington, Samuel P. 1973. "Transnational Organizations and World Politics." *World Politics* 25:333–68.

Huntley, Wade L. 1996. "Kant's Third Image: Systemic Sources of the Liberal Peace." *International Studies Quarterly* 40:45–76.

Jackman, Robert W. 1993. *Power without Force*. Ann Arbor: University of Michigan Press.

Jervis, Robert. 1991–92. "The Future of World Politics: Will It Resemble the Past?" *International Security* 16:39–73.

Kacowicz, Arie M. 1995. "Pluralistic Security Communities in the Third World? The Intriguing Cases of South America and West Africa." Paper presented at the annual meeting of the International Studies Association, 21–25 February, Chicago.

Kapstein, Ethan B. 1991. "We *are* US: The Myth of the Multinational." *National Interest* 26:55–62.

Kegley, Charles W. Jr. 1992. "The New Global Order: The Power of Principle in a Pluralist World." *Ethics and International Affairs* 6:21–40.

———, ed. 1995. *Controversies in International Relations Theory: Realism and the Neoliberal Challenge*. New York: St. Martin's.

Kegley, Charles W. Jr., and Margaret G. Hermann. 1995. "The Political Psychology of Peace through Democratization." *Cooperation and Conflict* 30:5–30.

Kegley, Charles W. Jr., and Gregory A. Raymond. 1990. *When Trust Breaks Down: Alliance Norms and World Politics*. Columbia: University of South Carolina Press.

———. 1994. *A Multipolar Peace? Great Power Politics in the Twenty-first Century*. New York: St. Martin's Press.

Kelman, Herbert C., and V. Lee Hamilton. 1989. *Crimes of Obedience*. New Haven, CT: Yale University Press.

Kennedy, Paul. 1987. *The Rise and Fall of the Great Powers*. New York: Random House.

Kennedy, Paul, and Bruce Russett. 1995. "Reforming the United Nations: Problems and Possibilities." *Foreign Affairs* 74:56–71.

Keohane, Robert O. 1984. *After Hegemony.* Princeton, NJ: Princeton University Press.

———. 1989. "Reciprocity in International Relations." In R. O. Keohane, ed., *International Institutions and State Power.* Boulder, CO: Westview.

Keohane, Robert O., Michael McGinnis, and Elinor Ostrom, eds. 1993. *Proceedings of a Conference on Linking Local and Global Commons.* Cambridge: Harvard University Center for International Affairs.

Keohane, Robert O., and Joseph S. Nye, eds. 1972. *Transnational Relations and World Politics.* Cambridge: Harvard University Press.

———. 1974. "Transnational Relations and International Organization." *World Politics* 27:39–62.

———. 1989. *Power and Interdependence.* 2d ed. Glenview, IL: Scott, Foresman.

Keohane, Robert O., and Elinor Ostrom, eds. 1995. *Local Commons and Global Interdependence.* London: Sage.

Kilgour, D. Marc. 1991. "Domestic Political Structure and War: A Game-Theoretic Approach." *Journal of Conflict Resolution* 35:266–84.

Kindleberger, Charles P. 1981. "Dominance and Leadership in the International Economy." *International Studies Quarterly* 25:242–54.

Kobrin, Stephen J. 1991. "An Empirical Analysis of the Determinants of Global Integration." *Strategic Management Journal* 12:17–32.

———. 1997. "Transnational Integration, National Markets and Nation-States." In Brian Toyne and Douglas Nigh, eds., *International Business: Emerging Issues and Opportunities.* Columbia: University of South Carolina Press.

Krasner, Stephen D. 1983. "Structural Causes and Regimes Consequences: Regimes as Intervening Variables." In Stephen Krasner, ed., *International Regimes.* Ithaca, NY: Cornell University Press.

Kratochwil, Friedrich, and John Ruggie. 1986. "International Organization: A State of the Art on an Art of the State." *International Organization* 40:753–75.

Kuhlman, James A. 1997. "The Levels of Analysis Problem Again: Community and Regionalism in the Global Political Economy." In Brian Toyne and Douglas Nigh, eds., *International Business: Emerging Issues and Opportunities.* Columbia: University of South Carolina Press.

Lave, Charles A., and James G. March. 1975. *An Introduction to Models in the Social Sciences.* New York: Harper and Row.

Layne, Christopher. 1994. "Kant or Cant: The Myth of Democratic Peace." *International Security* 19:5–49.

Lijphart, Arend. 1981. "Karl W. Deutsch and the New Paradigm in International Relations." In Richard L. Merritt and Bruce M. Russett, eds., *From National Development to Global Community.* London: George Allen and Unwin.

Mann, Michael. 1988. *States, War, and Capitalism.* Oxford: Blackwell.

Maoz, Zeev, and N. Abdolali. 1989. "Regime Types and International Conflict, 1816–1976." *Journal of Conflict Resolution* 33:3–35.

Maoz, Zeev, and Bruce Russett. 1992. "Alliances, Contiguity, Wealth, and Political Stability: Is the Lack of Conflict among Democracies a Statistical Arti-fact?" *International Interactions* 17:245–67.

———. 1993. "Normative and Structural Causes of the Democratic Peace." *American Political Science Review* 87:624–38.

McNeill, William H. 1982. *The Pursuit of Power.* Chicago: University of Chicago Press.

Miller, Gary, and Thomas Hammond. 1994. "Why Politics Is More Fundamental Than Economics: Incentive-Compatible Mechanisms Are Not Credible." *Journal of Theoretical Politics* 6:5–20.

Mintz, Alex, and Nehemiah Geva. 1995. "Why Don't Democracies Fight Each Other?: An Experimental Study." *Journal of Conflict Resolution* 37:484–503.

Morgan, T. Clifton, and S. H. Campbell. 1991. "Domestic Structure, Decisional Constraints, and War: So Why Kant Democracies Fight?" *Journal of Conflict Resolution* 35:187–211.

Morgan, T. Clifton, and Valerie L. Schwebach. 1992. "Take Two Democracies and Call Me in the Morning: A Prescription for Peace?" *International Interactions* 17:305–20.

Morgenthau, Hans J. 1973. *Politics among Nations.* 5th ed. New York: Alfred A. Knopf.

Most, Benjamin A., and Harvey Starr. 1989. *Inquiry, Logic and International Politics.* Columbia: University of South Carolina Press.

Mueller, John. 1989. *Retreat from Doomsday.* New York: Basic Books.

———. 1994. "The Catastrophe Quota: Trouble after the Cold War." *Journal of Conflict Resolution* 38:355–75.

———. 1995. *Quiet Cataclysm: Reflections on the Recent Transformation of World Politics.* New York: HarperCollins.

Nigh, Douglas. 1997. "Who's on First: Nation-States, National Identity, and Multinational Corporations." In Brian Toyne and Douglas Nigh, eds., *International Business: Emerging Issues and Opportunities.* Columbia: University of South Carolina Press.

Nijman, Jan. 1993. *The Geopolitics of Power and Conflict.* London: Belhaven.

North, Robert C., and Nazli Choucri. 1983. "Economic and Political Factors in International Conflict and Integration." *International Studies Quarterly* 27:443–61.

Nye, Joseph S., and Robert O. Keohane. 1971. "Transnational Relations and World Politics: An Introduction." *International Organization* 25:329–49.

Olson, Mancur. 1968. *The Logic of Collective Action.* New York: Schocken Books.

———. 1982. *The Rise and Decline of Nations.* New Haven, CT: Yale University Press.

Olson, Mancur, and Richard Zeckhauser. 1966. "An Economic Theory of Alliances." *Review of Economics and Statistics* 46:266–79.

Oneal, John R., Frances H. Oneal, Zeev Maoz, and Bruce Russett. 1996. "The Liberal Peace: Interdependence, Democracy, and International Conflict, 1950–85." *Journal of Peace Research* 33:11–28.

Ostrom, Elinor. 1990. *Governing the Commons.* Cambridge: Cambridge University Press.

Ostrom, Vincent, and Elinor Ostrom. 1977. "A Theory for Institutional Analysis of Common Pool Problems." In Garrett Hardin and John Baden, eds., *Managing the Commons.* San Francisco: W. H. Freeman.

Oye, Kenneth A. 1986. "Explaining Cooperation under Anarchy: Hypotheses and Strategies." In Kenneth Oye, ed., *Cooperation under Anarchy.* Princeton, NJ: Princeton University Press.

Puchala, Donald. 1981. "Integration Theory and the Study of International Relations." In Richard L. Merritt and Bruce M. Russett, eds., *From National Development to Global Community.* London: George Allen and Unwin.

Puchala, Donald J., and Roger A. Coate. 1989. *The Challenge of Relevance: The United Nations in a Changing World Environment.* New York: Academic Council on the United Nations System.

Putnam, Robert. 1993. "Democracy, Development, and the Civic Community: Evidence from an Italian Experiment." In Robert O. Keohane, Michael D. McGinnis, and Elinor Ostrom, eds., *Proceedings of a Conference on Linking Local and Global Commons.* Cambridge: Harvard University Center for International Affairs.

Rapoport, Anatol. 1960. *Fights, Games, and Debates.* Ann Arbor: University of Michigan Press.

Ray, James Lee. 1989. "The Abolition of Slavery and the End of International War." *International Organization* 43:405–39.

———. 1993. "Wars between Democracies: Rare, or Nonexistent?" *International Interactions* 18:251–76.

———. 1995. *Democracy and International Conflict.* Columbia: University of South Carolina Press.

Raymond, Gregory A. 1994. "Democracy, Disputes, and Third-Party Intermediaries," *Journal of Conflict Resolution* 38:24–42.

Reich, Robert B. 1990. "Who Is US?" *Harvard Business Review,* January-February, 53–64.

———. 1991. "Who Is Them?" *Harvard Business Review,* March-April, 77–88.

Richardson, Lewis F. 1960. *Statistics of Deadly Quarrels.* Chicago: Quadrangle Books.

Rochester, J. Martin. 1993. *Waiting for the Millennium: The United Nations and the Future of World Order.* Columbia: University of South Carolina Press.

Rosecrance, Richard. 1963. *Action and Reaction in World Politics.* Boston: Little, Brown.

Rosenau, James N. 1980. "Thinking Theory Thoroughly." In J. N. Rosenau, ed., *The Scientific Study of Foreign Policy.* Rev. ed. London: Frances Pinter.

———. 1990. *Turbulence in World Politics.* Princeton, NJ: Princeton University Press.

———. 1995. "Governance in the Twenty-first Century." *Global Governance* 1:13–43.

Rosenau, James N., and Ernst-Otto Czempiel, eds. 1992. *Governance without Government: Order and Change in World Politics.* Cambridge: Cambridge University Press.

Rummel, Rudolph J. 1968. "The Relationship between National Attributes and Foreign Conflict Behavior." In J. David Singer, ed., *Quantitative International Politics.* New York: Free Press.

———. 1983. "Libertarianism and International Violence." *Journal of Conflict Resolution* 27:27–71.

———. 1995. "Democracy, Power, Genocide, and Mass Murder." *Journal of Conflict Resolution* 39:3–26.

Russett, Bruce. 1963. *Community and Contention: Britain and America in the Twentieth Century.* Cambridge: MIT Press.

———. 1972. "A Macroscopic View of International Politics." In James N. Rosenau, Vincent Davis, and M. A. East, eds., *The Analysis of International Politics.* New York: Free Press.

———. 1983. "International Interactions and Processes: The Internal vs. External Debate Revisited." In Ada W. Finifter, ed., *Political Science: The State of the Discipline.* Washington, DC: American Political Science Association.

———. 1985. "The Mysterious Case of Vanishing Hegemony; or, Is Mark Twain Really Dead?" *International Organization* 39:207–31.

———. 1987. "Economic Change as a Cause of International Conflict." In C. Schmidt and F. Blackaby, eds., *Peace, Defence, and Economic Analysis.* London: Macmillan.

———. 1990. "Politics and Alternative Security: Toward a More Democratic, Therefore More Peaceful, World." In Burns H. Weston, ed., *Alternative Security: Living without Nuclear Deterrence.* Boulder, CO: Westview.

———. 1993a. "Can a Democratic Peace Be Built? *International Interactions* 18:277–82.

———. 1993b. *Grasping the Democratic Peace.* Princeton, NJ: Princeton University Press.

Russett, Bruce, and Harvey Starr. 1992. *World Politics: The Menu for Choice.* 4th ed. New York: W. H. Freeman.

———. 1996. *World Politics: The Menu for Choice.* 5th ed. New York: W. H. Freeman.

Russett, Bruce M., and John D. Sullivan. 1971. "Collective Goods and International Organizations." *International Organization* 25:845–65.

Russett, Bruce, and James S. Sutterlin. 1991. "The U.N. in a New World Order." *Foreign Affairs* 70:69–83.

Sandler, Todd. 1993. "The Economic Theory of Alliances." *Journal of Conflict Resolution* 37:446–83.

Sandler, Todd M., William Loehr, and Jon T. Cauley. 1978. *The Public Economy of Public Goods and International Cooperation.* Monograph Series in World Affairs, vol. 15. Denver: University of Denver.

Scharpf, Fritz W. 1994. "Games Real Actors Could Play: Positive and Negative Coordination in Embedded Negotiations." *Journal of Theoretical Politics* 6:27–53.

Schmookler, Andrew Bard. 1984. *The Parable of the Tribes.* Boston: Houghton Mifflin.

Schwartz, Herman M. 1994. *States Versus Markets.* New York: St. Martin's Press.

Shimko, Keith L. 1992. "Realism, Neoliberalism, and American Liberalism." *Review of Politics* 54:281–301.

Simon, Marc V., and Harvey Starr. 1996. "Extraction, Allocation, and the Rise and Decline of States." *Journal of Conflict Resolution* 40:272–97.

Singer, Max, and Aaron Wildavsky. 1993. *The Real World Order.* Chatham, NJ: Chatham House.

Siverson, Randolph M., and Julianne Emmons. 1991. "Birds of a Feather: Democratic Political Systems and Alliance Choices in the Twentieth Century." *Journal of Conflict Resolution* 35:285–306.

Siverson, Randolph M., and Ross Miller. 1991. "Democracy and the Escalation of Conflict." Paper presented at the annual meeting of the American Political Science Association, August 29–September 1, Washington, DC.

Siverson, Randolph M., and Harvey Starr. 1991. *The Diffusion of War.* Ann Arbor: University of Michigan Press.

———. 1992. "Regime Change and the Restructuring of Foreign Policy." Paper presented at the conference on Linkages Between National and International Politics, University of California, Davis, May 8–9.

Small, Melvin, and J. David Singer. 1976. "The War-Proneness of Democratic Regimes." *Jerusalem Journal of International Relations* 1:50–69.

Snidal, Duncan. 1985. "Coordination versus Prisoners' Dilemma: Implications for International Cooperation and Regimes." *American Political Science Review* 79:923–42.

———. 1995. "The Politics of Scope: Endogenous Actors, Heterogeneity and Institutions." In Robert O. Keohane and Elinor Ostrom, eds., *Local Commons and Global Interdependence.* London: Sage.

Snyder, Glenn H. 1971. "'Prisoner's Dilemma' and 'Chicken' Models in International Politics." *International Studies Quarterly* 15:66–103.

Soroos, Marvin S. 1986. *Beyond Sovereignty.* Columbia: University of South Carolina Press.

Spiro, David. 1994. "The Insignificance of the Liberal Peace." *International Security* 19:50–86.

Sprout, Harold, and Margaret Sprout. 1969. "Environmental Factors in the Study of International Politics." In James N. Rosenau, ed., *International Politics and Foreign Policy,* rev.ed. New York: Free Press.

Starr, Harvey. 1972. *War Coalitions.* Lexington, MA: D.C. Heath.

———. 1974. "A Collective Goods Analysis of the Warsaw Pact after Czechoslovakia," *International Organization* 28:521–32.

———. 1991a. "Joining Political and Geographic Perspectives: Geopolitics and International Relations." *International Interactions* 17:1–9.

———. 1991b. Review of *Turbulence in World Politics,* by James N. Rosenau. *Journal of Politics* 53:924–26.

———. 1991c. "Democratic Dominoes: Diffusion Approaches to the Spread of

Democracy in the International System." *Journal of Conflict Resolution* 35:356–81.

———. 1994. "Revolution and War: Rethinking the Linkage Between Internal and External Conflict." *Political Research Quarterly* 47:481–507.

———. 1995. "D2: The Diffusion of Democracy Revisited." Paper presented at the annual meeting of the International Studies Association, February 21–25, Chicago.

Stedman, Stephen John. 1993. "The New Interventionists." *Foreign Affairs* 72:1–16.

Stein, Arthur A. 1983. "Coordination and Collaboration: Regimes in an Anarchic World." In Stephen D. Krasner, ed., *International Regimes*. Ithaca, NY: Cornell University Press.

———. 1990. *Why Nations Cooperate*. Ithaca, NY: Cornell University Press.

Strang, David. 1991. "Global Patterns of Decolonization, 1500–1987." *International Studies Quarterly* 35:429–54.

Strange, Susan. 1983. "*Cave! hic dragones:* A Critique of Regime Analysis." In Stephen D. Krasner, ed., *International Regimes*. Ithaca, NY: Cornell University Press.

Taylor, Michael, and Sara Singleton. 1993. "The Communal Resource: Transaction Costs and the Solution of Collective Action Problems." In Robert O. Keohane, Michael D. McGinnis, and Elinor Ostrom, eds., *Proceedings of a Conference on Linking Local and Global Commons*. Cambridge: Harvard University Center for International Affairs.

Thies, Wallace J. 1987. "Alliances and Collective Goods: A Reappraisal." *Journal of Conflict Resolution* 31:298–332.

Tilly, Charles. 1975. "Reflections on the History of European State-Making." In Charles Tilly, ed., *The Formation of National States in Western Europe*. Princeton, NJ: Princeton University Press.

———. 1990. *Coercion, Capital, and European States*. Oxford: Basil Blackwell.

Tsebelis, George. 1990. *Nested Games*. Berkeley: University of California Press.

von Glahn, Gerhard. 1981. *Law among Nations*. 4th ed. New York: Macmillan.

———. 1992. *Law among Nations*. 7th ed. New York: Macmillan.

Waltz, Kenneth N. 1959. *Man, the State, and War*. New York: Columbia University Press.

———. 1979. *Theory of International Politics*. Reading, MA: Addison-Wesley.

Ward, Michael D., and Lewis L. House. 1988. "A Theory of the Behavioral Power of Nations." *Journal of Conflict Resolution* 32:3–36.

Weede, Erich. 1984. "Democracy and War Involvement." *Journal of Conflict Resolution* 28:649–64.

Wendt, Alexander E. 1987. "The Agent-Structure Problem in International Relations Theory." *International Organization* 41:337–70.

Wijkman, Per Magnus. 1982. "Managing the Global Commons." *International Organization* 36:511–36.

Young, Oran. 1980. "International Regimes: Problems of Concept Formation." *World Politics* 32:331–56.

Zacher, Mark W. 1992. "The Decaying Pillars of the Westphalian Temple: Implications for International Order and Governance." In James N. Rosenau and Ernst-Otto Czempiel, eds., *Governance without Government: Order and Change in World Politics.* Cambridge: Cambridge University Press.

Zacher, Mark W., and Richard A. Matthew. 1995. "Liberal International Theory: Common Threads, Divergent Strands." In C. W. Kegley, ed., *Controversies in International Relations Theory.* New York: St. Martin's.

Index